EAT COOL

GOOD FOOD FOR HOT DAYS

To my husband, Jon, and anyone else who finds hot and humid weather, in his words, soul-crushing.

EAT COOL
GOOD FOOD FOR HOT DAYS

First published in the United States of America in 2021 by
Rizzoli International Publications, Inc.
300 Park Avenue South
New York, NY 10010
rizzoliusa.com

© 2021 by Vanessa Seder
vanessaseder.com

Photography by Stacey Cramp
staceycramp.com

Design by Jennifer S. Muller
jennifermullerdesign.com

Relish&Co.
relishandco.com

Pages 4, 7, 21, 24, 99, and 103: Stoneware bowls and plates
courtesy of East Fork Pottery, Asheville, NC.
eastfork.com.

Publisher: Charles Miers
Editor: Jono Jarrett
Production Manager: Colin Hough-Trapp
Managing Editor: Lynn Scrabis

Printed in China
2021 2022 2023 2024 / 10 9 8 7 6 5 4 3 2

ISBN: 978-0-8478-6994-7
Library of Congress Control Number: 2020941311

Visit us online:
Facebook.com/RizzoliNewYork
Twitter: @Rizzoli_Books
Instagram.com/RizzoliBooks
Pinterest.com/RizzoliBooks
Youtube.com/user/RizzoliNY

EAT COOL

GOOD FOOD FOR HOT DAYS

100 Easy, Satisfying,
and Refreshing Recipes that
Won't Heat Up Your Kitchen

Vanessa Seder

CONTENTS

INTRODUCTION

"IN THIS HEAT EVERY EXTRA GESTURE WAS AN AFFRONT TO THE COMMON STORE OF LIFE."
—F. SCOTT FITZGERALD, *THE GREAT GATSBY*

In the depths of a prolonged hot spell, the mere thought of figuring out what to eat can fill any cook with anxiety and fatigue. Who can be blamed for taking the path of least resistance and settling for whatever food option requires the minimum of attention and effort? The reality, though, is that the way we cook and eat dramatically affects our mood and sense of well-being—and this goes double when our internal radiators are on the verge of boiling over. At such times, in fact, a thoughtful approach to feeding ourselves and our families can be the difference between lethargy, ill temper, and discomfort on one hand and composure, alertness, and productivity on the other.

The objective of *Eat Cool* is to provide such an approach. It is a fun, versatile guidebook and collection of tried and tested recipes for cooks of all levels to expand their range of options and personal culinary tool kit. In these pages you'll find a family-friendly array of creative and delicious meals, snacks, drinks, and desserts based on smart ingredients to keep your body from overheating; dozens of achievable, make-ahead dishes that can be served cold or at room temperature; and a variety of no-heat techniques and principles that will keep your fridge stocked with items ideal for quick assembly of satisfying meals. (If you happen to learn a thing or two about using local, seasonal ingredients along the way, so much the better.)

Astute readers will note Asian, Indian, South American, Mexican, Middle Eastern, and Mediterranean influences throughout. Not only are these cuisines among my very favorites—they're also rich sources of climate-savvy culinary wisdom, having evolved over thousands of years in hot and humid regions. Accordingly, I've drawn liberally from them and emulated certain approaches,

such as drinking hot tea (see the Sweet Lemongrass-Ginger Tea on page 193) and eating spicy foods, including the Spicy Papaya Slaw (page 61), Pasta with Crab, Herbs, and Chiles (page 139), and Spicy Daikon Pickles (page 223).

While I believe food should be beautiful and visually pleasing, *Eat Cool* is meant not as an aspirational or coffee table cookbook, but rather as real, working manual—which I hope will become well worn and food-stained over time. Nor is it an activist's manual, although it can be part of any family's broader approach to eating more seasonally and sustainably or to lowering energy use during hot weather.

To this end, all recipes included in *Eat Cool* meet the following criteria:

1. IS IT DELICIOUS AND ENJOYABLE TO EAT?
Seems simple, right? First and foremost is a variety of contrasting yet complementary flavors, textures, colors, and temperatures. Broadly, cold recipes must be more brightly flavored, well balanced, and thoroughly seasoned than dishes served hot. The Cold Carrot, Cashew, and Ginger Soup (page 86), for example, infuses crunch, salt, and heat via add-ins such as hot, olive oil–fried carrot leaves and crunchy spices. Another example is the fun-to-slurp Glass Noodle Salad with Pork, Cucumber, and Lemongrass (page 79), which offsets sizzling meat with cold and crunchy vegetables, herbs, and spices, tossed with slippery noodles and a vibrant dressing. I also made a point of choosing fruits and vegetables in season during the summer months, for the obvious reason that seasonal produce is superior in flavor, aroma, texture, and appearance—see the Fresh Corn Salad with Peas and Herbs on page 63.

2. WILL IT KEEP YOU RELATIVELY COOL?

To eat cool does not mean giving up meat, dairy, or rich foods, but duty compels me to report that you'll find relief from the heat if you eat them more selectively and boost the proportion of vegetables, fruits, and grains in your diet. These are less work for your body to digest. Many recipes in this book, therefore, are lower in fat and plant based—and those that call for animal-based protein use cuts of meat that don't need to be cooked long (which also keeps your kitchen cooler). *Eat Cool* can help you learn to eat this way painlessly, thanks to its abundant use of fresh and cooling ingredients like yogurt, cucumbers, herbs, greens, citrus, ice, aloe vera, vinegar, melon, and berries.

3. DOES IT AVOID THE NEED FOR LOTS OF LABOR AND COOKING?

While the recipes in this book inevitably vary somewhat with respect to both labor-intensiveness and cooking time, I've selected ingredients and techniques throughout that should minimize both. The Grilled Marinated Skirt Steak and Barley Salad with Dried Cherries, Fresh Herbs, and Lemon Pickle (page 149), for example, cooks quickly on the grill. For dishes with pasta and grains, some shapes or varieties take less time to cook, such as the rice noodles in the Cold Korean-Style Vegetable Noodles with Gochujang and Kimchi (page 131) that finish in just three to four minutes. Other techniques to hasten the cooking process include cutting food small to maximize surface area, such as in the Grilled Chicken and Sweet Potato Street Tacos with Radish, Pickled Red Cabbage, and Black Beans (page 141). For those soups that do require cooking, such as Cauliflower, Pea, and Leek Soup Topped with Heirloom Tomatoes, Pea Tendrils, and Olive Oil (page 91), sweating vegetables and other ingredients in a covered pot over low heat develops flavor without the need for hours of stovetop simmering.

Finally, for those occasions when temperatures are at their most infernal, you'll find a multitude of recipes that take very little time to throw together and even avoid the need for cooking entirely—such as the Melon and Cucumber Breakfast Salad (page 20), Shaved Salad in Creamy Tahini Dressing (page 64), and Scallop Ceviche with Lime, Avocado, Cilantro, and Chiles (page 42), plus tips on creating family-friendly meals from tinned seafood (see page 120) and purchased rotisserie chicken (see page 147). Starting on page 214, you'll

find flavorful condiments, pickles, and sauces designed to help you develop an arsenal of pantry items to add to salads, simple proteins, and precooked grains for instant meals.

4. CAN THE HOME CHEF MAKE IT SUCCESSFULLY?

As a cooking instructor, I believe that cooking is a life skill everyone should have. Being self-sufficient in the kitchen is quite liberating. Accordingly, *Eat Cool* recipes are written to be approachable and realistic for the busy home cook to make, with a bias toward avoiding anything fussy or complicated (any recipe I wasn't sure about was tested by friends, neighbors, or colleagues during the summer months to make sure it was achievable and written clearly enough to follow). Many of the recipes have elements that can be prepped in advance (in hot weather, I suggest using the early morning for this). You'll be amazed how much easier it is to produce a meal (and entertain) when all you have to do is assemble its components. For example, when making the Poke Bowls with Pickled Bok Choy, Hijiki, and Marinated Shiitake Mushrooms over Sushi Rice (page 126), you can pickle the bok choy and ginger and marinate the mushrooms well ahead of time. When dinnertime comes, all that's left to do is slice the tuna and make the rice.

5. ARE ITS INGREDIENTS EASY TO FIND (OR CAN VIABLE SUBSTITUTIONS BE PROVIDED)?

The recipes in this book are based on ingredients that can be readily found across the country—for the most part, at least. As noted, *Eat Cool* pulls from global influences, so some recipes may send you to the international aisle of your supermarket or a specialty market for the more exotic ingredients. I also offer alternative suggestions for items that may be hard to find or have a short season. While I encourage you to try your local market first, it's worth remembering that in this day and age, you can order practically anything online.

I could go on and on about this topic, but let me stop there. It's time to take a deep breath and jump in—or dip in your pinky toe if you're the cautious sort. Remember, just because it's hot enough out there to fry an egg on the sidewalk doesn't mean you have to settle for sidewalk eggs! The many alternatives this book offers will help you stay cool, calm, and collected—and happily fed—until that blessed heat finally lifts. *Eat cool* and be happy.

BREAKFAST

MOCK VANILLA MILKSHAKE

SERVES 2 TO 4 | ACTIVE TIME: 8 MINUTES | TOTAL TIME: 8 MINUTES

This delicious, cold, frothy, and healthy smoothie came about a year or so ago one morning when our daughter announced a new addition to her never-ending list of extremely specific dietary rules and requirements. She no longer liked colorful smoothies, she informed us matter-of-factly—just white ones. (Based on the same principle that preachers' kids are often hell-raisers, it seems, chefs' offspring tend to be ultra-finicky eaters.) I suppose most parenting manuals would frown upon giving in to such demands, but I found myself intrigued by—and unable to resist—the white smoothie challenge. Frankly, I regard any smoothie she asks for as a plus since I can sneak in nutritious stuff she'd never touch otherwise. Chia, hemp, and flax seeds are all excellent sources of omega-3 fatty acids, fiber, and protein, and once blended with the bananas, dates, and vanilla, all three seeds magically disappear into the white froth of the smoothie. Operating under the age-old principle that lying is wrong unless it helps get your kids to eat healthy, I dubbed the resulting concoction the Mock Vanilla Milkshake, figuring that this would have a more appealing ring to a five-year-old's ears than Chia, Hemp, and Flax Smoothie. The joke turned out to be on me, though. While she normally turns her nose up at unfamiliar things, she actually loves to help me make this smoothie, and even adds the chia, flax, and hemp herself. As long as the resulting smoothie is white, slightly sweet, creamy, and tastes of vanilla, her palate can accommodate it, apparently. Where's the logic here?!

2 whole frozen peeled bananas, cut into 1-inch pieces

2 pitted Medjool dates

2 tablespoons almond flour

1 teaspoon chia seeds

1 teaspoon flax seeds

1 teaspoon hemp seeds

2 cups whole cow's milk or plain unsweetened almond milk

2 teaspoons pure vanilla extract

¾ cup ice cubes

Place the bananas, dates, almond flour, chia seeds, flax seeds, hemp seeds, milk, vanilla, and ice in a blender.

Blend on low speed until the fruit is finely chopped, about 1 minute, then blend on high speed until rich and frothy, about 1 more minute. Divide between glasses. Serve immediately.

NO-BAKE ALMOND BUTTER, CHERRY, DARK CHOCOLATE, AND MARCONA ALMOND GRANOLA BARS

MAKES 12 | ACTIVE TIME: 15 MINUTES | TOTAL TIME: 1 HOUR 25 MINUTES

Made with dark chocolate, tart dried cherries, and salty Marcona almonds, these crispy, chewy, sweet-and-salty, almond-buttery bars are a great option for a hearty snack, breakfast on-the-go, or even crumbled over yogurt or ice cream for a simple and easy dessert.

The dry ingredients then get bound together with a flavorful combination of almond butter, brown rice syrup (a natural sweetener that's milder than honey or sugar), and coconut oil for just a hint of coconut flavor. Marcona almonds hail from Spain. Shorter and rounder than your everyday almond, Marconas are blanched to remove the skin, then roasted in olive oil and salt. They serve double duty in these bars, providing both a hit of protein and a delectable roasty flavor, no oven required.

1½ cups old-fashioned rolled oats

1 cup puffed brown rice cereal

½ cup dried pitted unsweetened cherries

½ cup roughly chopped Marcona almonds

¼ cup natural smooth almond butter

½ cup brown rice syrup

¼ cup virgin (unrefined) coconut oil

¼ teaspoon ground cinnamon

¼ teaspoon sea salt

1 teaspoon pure vanilla extract

⅓ cup chopped dark chocolate

Line an 8-inch square baking pan with parchment paper and set aside.

In a large bowl, stir together the oats, brown rice cereal, cherries, and almonds. Set aside.

Combine the almond butter, brown rice syrup, coconut oil, cinnamon, and salt in a small saucepan over medium heat and cook, stirring occasionally, until the coconut oil melts and the mixture thins slightly, about 4 minutes. Turn off the heat and stir in the vanilla.

Pour the almond butter mixture over the oat mixture and gently stir to combine and coat. Let cool slightly, about 5 minutes, then stir in the chocolate.

Spread the mixture out evenly into the prepared pan, cover with parchment paper, and use your hands to press down into the pan, creating a flat, even layer.

Transfer to the refrigerator until set, about 1 hour, then slice into 12 bars. The finished bars can be stored in an airtight container or individually wrapped in wax paper and kept in the refrigerator for up to 1 week.

BUTTERMILK NECTARINE MUESLI

SERVES 4 | ACTIVE TIME: 12 MINUTES | TOTAL TIME: 8 HOURS

Muesli is a soft and mushy (in a good way) cold cereal of Swiss-German origin, usually made with a mixture of nuts, grains, and fruits and softened with a liquid such as milk, almond milk, fruit juice, or yogurt. I sometimes think of it as a soft, unbaked, refrigerated version of granola. Another good softening agent is buttermilk. Name notwithstanding, buttermilk contains no butter—it's simply a cultured milk product. I like the added tanginess it infuses the grains with as it tenderizes and softens them. The slightly sweet grainy flavor of the wheat germ and oat bran is also a nice contrast to the tangy buttermilk and sweet honey. I've paired the mixture here with nectarines and dried apricots to capitalize on their sweet, floral flavor. Ripe nectarines should feel slightly soft and smell at least a little sweet. If yours aren't ready, feel free to substitute other ripe seasonal fruits such as plums, apricots, cherries, or berries. This recipe requires time for the softening effect to occur, so make this the night before to ensure it's ready to eat by the time the rooster crows.

1½ **cups raw rolled oats**

½ **cup wheat germ**

¼ **cup oat bran**

½ **cup chopped raw almonds**

5 nectarines, 3 peeled and sliced, 2 chopped for garnish

¼ **cup honey**

1 cup buttermilk

1 teaspoon pure vanilla extract

½ **teaspoon sea salt**

¼ **cup finely chopped crystalized ginger**

½ **cup finely chopped dried apricots**

Place the rolled oats, wheat germ, oat bran, and almonds in a medium bowl and stir to combine.

Place the 3 sliced nectarines, the honey, buttermilk, vanilla, and salt in a blender and blend on high speed until smooth and frothy, about 2 minutes.

Pour the buttermilk mixture over the oat mixture, stir to coat, then cover and refrigerate at least 8 hours or overnight, until the muesli has softened and has the consistency of thick oatmeal.

Stir the ginger and apricots into the muesli, then spoon into bowls and top with the chopped nectarines. The muesli can be stored in the refrigerator for up to 2 days.

SUMMER FRUIT, APPLE, AND PEPITA RAW BREAKFAST HODGEPODGE

SERVES 2 TO 4 | ACTIVE TIME: 10 MINUTES | TOTAL TIME: 20 MINUTES

This no-cook, coarsely ground fruit and pepita (pumpkin seed) "porridge," similar in consistency to cooked oatmeal, is a favorite for my husband and me. Ideal for starting the day off on the right foot when you're trying to eat healthier, it's also a great option when you don't feel like turning on any heat element yet need something more substantial than a smoothie. Lightly sweet, a touch salty, a little tart, and satisfyingly rich and crunchy, it relies on a base of ripe plums, berries, and apple, and is sweetened with dates and thickened with pumpkin and chia seeds. The latter of these has the virtue of bulking up and gel-ifying when mixed with liquid, contributing to the porridge's agreeably robust texture. The hodgepodge gets drizzled with olive oil, providing richness and a slightly grassy flavor that pleasantly complements the sweet fruit. Besides leaving you fuller longer than a mere fruit salad would, adding the seeds brings a variety of heroic nutritional benefits. Chia seeds, a superfood, are rich in fiber, omega-3s, antioxidants, potassium, and calcium. And the raw pumpkin seeds are no slouch either, as they are loaded with healthy fats, magnesium, and zinc. I advocate making this the evening before so that breakfast is ready by the time the sun peeks over the horizon.

½ cup raw hulled pepitas

1 tablespoon chia seeds

½ cup water

2 pitted Medjool dates

2 ripe plums, pitted and chopped, plus more for topping

1 Gala apple, peeled, cored, and chopped

1 cup hulled and chopped strawberries, plus more for topping

1 cup raspberries, plus more for topping

½ teaspoon sea salt

Extra virgin olive oil for drizzling

Place the pepitas, chia seeds, and water in the bowl of a food processor and let sit for about 10 minutes. This allows the chia seeds to begin their gelling process.

Add the dates and process until the dates and seeds are coarsely chopped, about 1 minute.

Add the plums, apple, strawberries, raspberries, and salt. Process, scraping the sides a few times with a rubber spatula if necessary, until pureed. Divide between bowls and top with more chopped fruit and a drizzle of olive oil. Serve immediately, or store in the refrigerator in an airtight container for up to 2 days (garnish just before serving).

PAPAYA, GINGER, AND LIME SMOOTHIE

SERVES 2 TO 4 | ACTIVE TIME: 10 MINUTES | TOTAL TIME: 10 MINUTES

This cool, Creamsicle-colored smoothie is a bracing, healthy, and delicious way to start a hot day. Satisfying without being too heavy, it features a mix of qualities not unlike those of the mango lassi found at many Indian restaurants. These include fruitiness from the papaya, sweetness from honey, and tanginess from the lime and yogurt. The yogurt also provides a sense of substance and creaminess, and there's also a bit of heat, courtesy of the ginger. The resulting elixir will add some bounce to your morning gait, sweltering conditions be damned. Note: If you want it frosty, try freezing the papaya ahead of time (see page 168).

3 cups chopped fresh papaya (from one 3-pound ripe papaya that has been peeled, seeded, and cut into 1-inch dice)

1 cup whole milk plain yogurt

1½ teaspoons grated fresh ginger

3 tablespoons honey

1 teaspoon fresh lime zest, plus more (optional) for garnish

1 tablespoon fresh lime juice

1 cup plain unsweetened almond milk

Pinch sea salt

In a high-powered blender, combine the papaya chunks, yogurt, ginger, honey, lime zest, lime juice, almond milk, and salt. Blend on low speed until the mixture begins to thin out, about 2 minutes, then blend on high speed until frothy, about 1 more minute.

Divide between glasses. Garnish with fresh lime zest, if desired. Serve immediately.

PASSION FRUIT, MANGO, AND COCONUT PARFAITS

SERVES 6 | ACTIVE TIME: 35 MINUTES | TOTAL TIME: 35 MINUTES

Comprised of layers of passion fruit curd, mango puree, and cooling coconut yogurt and topped with crunchy coconut chips, this tropical recipe is an edible sunrise worth getting out of bed early for. It makes for a quick, self-contained breakfast or a great, fresh finale for a brunch spread. This recipe requires some effort and time, so I often make it the night before and refrigerate; these parfaits will hold up nicely in the fridge for a few days—but don't be surprised if they disappear long before that. For the best textured whipped coconut cream, look for canned coconut milk that contains guar gum.

½ cup unsweetened passion fruit pulp, thawed if frozen

½ cup sugar

4 tablespoons unsalted butter, melted and cooled

5 large egg yolks

2½ cups chopped ripe mango (from 2 peeled and pitted mangos)

1 (13.5-ounce) can unsweetened coconut milk (made with guar gum)

1½ cups low-fat plain Greek yogurt

1 cup unsweetened coconut chips for sprinkling

Place the passion fruit pulp, sugar, butter, and egg yolks in a medium saucepan and stir until smooth. Heat over medium-low heat while stirring constantly until barely simmering and thickened, 8 to 10 minutes. The mixture should thicken before it reaches a boil. Use a silicone spatula to push the curd through a fine-mesh strainer into a medium stainless steel bowl. Place that bowl over a large bowl of ice water and stir until cool. Refrigerate until ready to use.

Place the mango in a high-powdered blender or food processor and process until smooth. Transfer the mixture to a large piping bag.

Use a can opener to open the can of coconut milk. Transfer about ½ cup of the thick cream layer from the top of the can into a medium bowl. Beat with a whisk until soft peaks form, then fold into the passion fruit curd. Transfer this mixture to a large piping bag, if desired.

In a medium bowl, whisk ½ cup coconut milk from the can with the Greek yogurt until smooth. Transfer this mixture to a large piping bag.

Set up 6 parfait or juice glasses wide enough to accommodate a spoon. Pipe or spoon layers of the mango puree, passion fruit curd, and yogurt into each glass. Serve immediately, or refrigerate up to 2 days ahead until ready to serve. Top each glass with coconut flakes right before serving.

MELON AND CUCUMBER BREAKFAST SALAD

SERVES 4 | ACTIVE TIME: 10 MINUTES | TOTAL TIME: 10 MINUTES

This sweet, savory, and mildly spicy salad, consisting of melon and cucumber drizzled with spicy honey dressing and fresh herbs, is a first-rate option when you wake up and it's already hot as blazes—that is, when turning on the stove or oven is out of the question and a lightweight morning meal with bright, summery notes is just what the doctor ordered. Just chop, whisk, and plate away. Here I've raised the stakes by serving with a dollop of Greek yogurt and (in case you need to impress high-rolling guests, in-laws, and/or visiting dignitaries), edible flowers.

Note: If this recipe floats your melon boat, think of it as a template that you can vary to your personal taste, using your preferred seasonal melon and a citrus/acid, sweetener, spice, creamy element, and herb of your choice.

1 (3- to 3½-pound) ripe cantaloupe or crenshaw melon

1 seedless cucumber, peeled and thinly sliced

3 tablespoons fresh lemon juice

1 tablespoon honey

½ teaspoon Aleppo chile flakes

1 tablespoon fresh lemon thyme or regular thyme leaves

⅓ cup extra virgin olive oil

½ teaspoon sea salt

¼ cup fresh mint leaves

¼ cup edible flowers, such as borage, marigold, or thyme

Freshly ground black pepper

Whole plain Greek yogurt (optional) for serving

Use a sharp chef's knife to cut the top and bottom off the melon so that it forms a flat surface. With the flat side down on a cutting board, cut around the sides of the melon, removing the peel and revealing the orange flesh.

Cut the melon in half and use a spoon to scoop out the seeds. Cut the melon into thin slices. Arrange the melon and cucumber on a large serving platter.

In a small bowl, whisk together the lemon juice and honey, Aleppo chile, thyme, olive oil, and salt. Spoon the dressing all over the sliced melon and cucumber.

Garnish with the mint leaves and edible flowers and sprinkle with black pepper. Serve with dollops of Greek yogurt, if desired. Serve immediately or refrigerate and serve within a few hours.

TAMAGO WITH RICE, SESAME SEEDS, AND PICKLED PLUM

SERVES 4 | ACTIVE TIME: 20 MINUTES | TOTAL TIME: 35 MINUTES

If you've eaten at a traditional sushi restaurant, you may have seen *tamago*—rectangles of rich, sweetened egg, usually lashed to a bite-sized bed of rice by a dark band of toasted seaweed. Essentially a sweet and savory Japanese omelet cooked in rich, aromatic sesame oil, a piece or two of *tamago nigari* is a fabulous way to end a sushi meal.

Because it can be served cold, I've found that tamago makes for a splendid hot weather breakfast in its own right. In this recipe I've paired sliced tamago omelet with *umeboshi*, a small pickled plum-like fruit that helps to cut through the richness of the tamago. You should be able to find the Japanese ingredients in this recipe at your local Asian market or the Asian section at your local supermarket. *Hondashi* is a powdered form of dashi broth made of bonito (dried smoked fish) and *kombu* (dried seaweed). Dashi broth, which gives the tamago its distinctive umami flavor, is used as a base for many Japanese dishes. For a vegetarian version (or *more* vegetarian, perhaps, given that eggs are front and center), you can leave the bonito out—it'll still taste great, if with a bit less umami.

Purists may insist that tamago must be prepared in a square-shaped tamago pan. Pay no mind: made in a round pan it tastes equally delicious (though the edges may lack the perfect right angles found in your local sushi house version). That said, I recently invested in a tamago pan, and it comes out right every single time, so if a) this recipe becomes a staple in your kitchen, or b) you're a perfectionist, you might consider making the investment.

Note: The process of forming the tamago log may sound complicated based on the description below. It isn't—it's just a bit hard to describe. Many tutorials and demonstration videos by sushi masters can be found on YouTube.

If you like, you can prepare the tamago the night before and refrigerate it so that in the morning you need only make the rice. If you're feeling inspired (or lazy), make extra rice to use for the *onigiri* on page 50 or the poke on page 126.

1½ cups sushi rice

3 tablespoons unseasoned rice vinegar

4 teaspoons sugar, divided

6 large eggs

1 teaspoon Hondashi granules

2 tablespoons mirin

1 teaspoon soy sauce or tamari

Canola oil

½ teaspoon toasted sesame oil

Toasted sesame seeds for serving

Shredded toasted seaweed for serving

Umeboshi plums for serving

Place the rice in a fine-mesh strainer and rinse under cold water until the water runs clear, then transfer to a medium saucepan. Cover with 2 cups water and bring to a simmer over high heat. Reduce the heat to low, cover, and cook until the liquid has absorbed, about 20 minutes. Immediately transfer the rice to a large bowl.

In a small bowl, stir together the rice vinegar and 2 teaspoons of the sugar until the sugar dissolves. Pour over the rice, stir to combine, and cover loosely with plastic wrap or a cloth until ready to eat. The rice can be served warm or at room temperature along with the tamago.

Meanwhile, in a medium bowl, whisk together the eggs, Hondashi, remaining 2 teaspoons sugar, the mirin, and soy sauce until pale yellow, about 2 minutes.

Heat a small cast-iron skillet or tamago pan over medium-low heat, about 2 minutes. Brush all over with canola oil, then pour in a thin layer of egg, just enough to fully cover the bottom of the pan in a thin sheet. Let cook until just set, 30 seconds to 1 minute, then use a large rubber spatula to fold the front edge of the egg—about an inch—toward the back of the omelet. Continue to roll (or flip) the closest edge toward the back of the pan until a log is formed on the far side of the skillet or pan (farthest away from you).

With the egg still in the skillet, brush the exposed area of the skillet with more oil. Add another few tablespoons of egg to cover the bottom of the pan while gently lifting the rolled egg up slightly so that the raw egg mixture can coat the pan underneath and will adhere to the bottom of the cooked portion as it cooks. Let the thin sheet of egg set slightly. This time you will be rolling from the back of the pan toward yourself, starting with the "already rolled" log. Use the rubber spatula to flip the log over the new egg and continue to "roll" from the back until you reach the front of the pan. When complete, slide the now larger "log" of rolled egg to the back of the pan. Repeat this process, rolling the egg as tightly as possible, until half of the egg mixture is used. The tamago should be rolled into a thick log shape, cooked through but still moist. Ideally the color will be golden yellow throughout (if the occasional light brown patch occurs, no worries, though).

Make a second tamago using the remaining egg mixture. Carefully transfer both logs of tamago to a plate. Use a pastry brush to lightly brush both all over with toasted sesame oil. Cover the warm tamagos with plastic wrap and refrigerate until just slightly warm, room temperature, or cold, depending on your preference.

To serve, place ¾ cup rice in each of the bottom of 4 bowls. Slice both tamago logs crosswise into ½-inch-thick slices and divide among the bowls. Sprinkle with sesame seeds and shredded seaweed and garnish with umeboshi. The tamagos can be made up to 1 day ahead of time and refrigerated until ready to slice and eat.

GREEN SHAKSHUKA

SERVES 4 | ACTIVE TIME: 25 MINUTES | TOTAL TIME: 40 MINUTES

Traditional North African shakshuka is started on the stovetop by cooking red peppers and onions (and sometimes tomatoes) with a bevy of spices. The mixture is topped with raw eggs and baked in the oven. Finally, the bubbling pan is brought to the table and served with bread for dipping. In my reworked shakshuka, green leafy vegetables, almonds, and chopped chiles form the base of the dish and are baked with the eggs from the get-go, no stovetop cooking necessary. If your objective is to cool off, the spicy heat from the serrano chile will induce sweating, so use as much as your taste buds can stand.

2 cloves garlic, peeled

3 tablespoons raw almonds

1 teaspoon fresh lemon zest

2 cups baby kale

2 cups baby spinach

1 cup baby arugula

1 cup fresh flat-leaf parsley leaves

1 cup fresh cilantro leaves

2 teaspoons chopped serrano chile, or more to taste

2 tablespoons fresh lemon juice

½ cup plus 1 tablespoon extra virgin olive oil

Sea salt

8 large eggs

Freshly ground black pepper

½ cup fresh basil leaves for serving

Flatbread or pita for serving

Preheat the oven to 400°F.

Combine the garlic, almonds, and lemon zest in the bowl of a food processor and process until finely chopped, about 1 minute.

Add the kale, spinach, arugula, parsley, cilantro, chile, lemon juice, and ½ cup of the olive oil and pulse until smooth, scraping the sides of the bowl if needed. Season with salt.

Spread the green vegetable sauce all over the bottom of a 4-quart shallow glass or ceramic baking dish. Use a spoon to gently form 8 wells in the sauce. Gently crack the eggs over each of the wells. Season the eggs with salt and pepper and drizzle with the remaining 1 tablespoon oil.

Place in the oven and bake until the egg whites are just set and the yolks are still slightly runny, 10 to 13 minutes. Remove from the oven and top with the basil leaves. Serve immediately with flatbread or pita for dipping.

FRISÉE WITH CRISPY OLIVE OIL-FRIED EGG AND HARISSA OIL

SERVES 4 | ACTIVE TIME: 12 MINUTES | TOTAL TIME: 12 MINUTES

This breakfast recipe packs a wallop—don't hesitate to slot it into your lunch or dinner rotation as well. The flavor and textural contrasts created by juxtaposing hot rich salty egg with spicy homemade harissa oil and cold, crisp, crunchy frisée will make your eaters sit up and take notice, possibly even salute. Frisée, the curly-leafed cousin of endive, is in the chicory family, which also includes radicchio and escarole—all hearty and slightly bitter greens that can hold up to rich and hot ingredients such as fried eggs, offering a captivating flavor balance without too much wilt. The harissa adds complexity and depth, with contributions of notes coming from the chiles (heat), caraway seeds (hints of North Africa), and coriander (earthiness). It looks pretty, too.

One of the distinct pleasures of this dish is the crispy edges on the fried egg—the reason olive oil is used here. If you love an extra-crispy fried egg, olive oil is always the way to go. Fats have different smoking points—that is, the temperature at which a fat starts to bubble, break down, and smoke. Using olive oil, with a higher smoking point than butter, allows your eggs to fry over a higher heat, which in turn allows your edges to crisp while the yolks remain soft and runny—ideal for coating the fine, curly leaves of your frisée.

Note: If you like the crispy-egg breakfast salad premise, this recipe can accommodate endless variations. Try experimenting with other greens, and don't hesitate to add in leftover odds and ends of your choosing for additional frugal/eco-friendly substance—think bacon lardons, roasted veggies, or stale-bread croutons.

2 cloves garlic, peeled and thinly sliced

½ cup extra virgin olive oil, divided

1 Fresno chile, stem removed and thinly sliced

¼ teaspoon caraway seeds

¼ teaspoon ground cumin

¼ teaspoon ground coriander

1 teaspoon red wine vinegar

Sea salt

Freshly ground black pepper

8 large eggs

6 cups frisée (from 1 or 2 heads), washed and dried, leaves torn

2 cups fresh cilantro sprigs for serving

Place the garlic and ¼ cup of the olive oil in a small skillet. Cook over medium-high heat until the garlic is just lightly golden, about 1 minute. Add the chile and caraway seeds and cook until the chile is soft, about 1 more minute.

Pour the mixture into a small bowl and let cool slightly. Stir in the cumin, coriander, and vinegar. Season with ½ teaspoon salt and ½ teaspoon black pepper. Set aside.

Divide the frisée among 4 plates. Set aside.

Heat 2 tablespoons of the remaining olive oil in a large cast-iron or nonstick skillet over medium-high heat. Once the oil is shimmering, crack in 4 eggs. Season the eggs with salt and pepper. Cook until the edges of the eggs are crispy and just turning brown, about 2 minutes. Cover with a lid just until the tops of the eggs are opaque but the yolks are still runny, about 1 more minute.

Transfer the eggs to 2 of the plates that have the frisée on them. Repeat with the remaining 4 eggs and remaining 2 plates with frisée. Drizzle the harissa oil over the tops of the eggs and frisée and garnish with cilantro sprigs. Serve immediately.

Any leftover harissa oil can be stored, refrigerated, in an airtight container for up to 1 week.

ESPRESSO CARDAMOM GRANITA

SERVES 4 TO 8 | ACTIVE TIME: 15 MINUTES | TOTAL TIME: 6 HOURS

I first heard of espresso granita when my husband returned home from a sweltering summer wedding in Sicily raving about it. Iced coffee for breakfast makes perfect sense, so I noted his description of an amped-up, sweet frozen version with dollops of whipped cream as something to try out myself. This version incorporates cardamom, an exotic flavor complement for the espresso that's less acidic than the usual lemon twist. Just remember that cardamom is highly floral and intense, so a little goes a long way.

Though a snap to make, granitas can be a bit time-intensive. The large and flaky ice crystals, perfect for scooping into a mug or dessert glass at one's leisure, are well worth the forking effort.

1 tablespoon instant espresso powder

¾ teaspoon ground cardamom

¾ cup sugar

3 cups freshly brewed strong hot coffee

2 teaspoons pure vanilla extract, divided

1 cup heavy cream, chilled

Whisk together the espresso powder, cardamom, and sugar in a medium bowl.

Add the fresh coffee and whisk until the sugar dissolves, then whisk in 1 teaspoon of the vanilla.

Pour the mixture into a 6-quart shallow container or an 8-inch square baking pan and carefully transfer to the freezer.

Freeze for 2 hours. Then use a fork to scrape up the ice crystals that form. Continue to scrape every hour until the mixture is completely frozen and has lovely large crystals, about 6 hours total.

In a large bowl, whisk the cream and the remaining 1 teaspoon vanilla until soft peaks form.

The granita can be kept in an airtight container in the freezer for up to 1 week. To serve, scoop the granita into 4 to 8 glasses and top with dollops of whipped cream.

OVERNIGHT COLD BREW

For those of us who depend on strong, good-quality coffee, the iced version, let's face it, is all too often a substandard diluted product that involves massive plastic cups, plastic straws, and as much ice as coffee. Copious amounts must be consumed in order to achieve one's desired caffeinated state. For me, there are two viable methods of addressing this matter. The first is to add an espresso shot or two to your iced coffee (aka the "iced red-eye"). That's well and good if you're in an air-conditioned café and a barista does the work. But who wants—or has the time—to double-grind, double-brew, and double-clean at home, especially when it's already hot out?

The second approach, the one I'm advocating here, is to cold-brew. You've probably noticed cold brew popping up ever more frequently at cafes and on restaurant menus. Sweeter, less acidic, and milder tasting than hot coffee, yet boasting a comparable caffeine jolt, cold brew eschews the usual quick-brew hot water process. Instead, finely ground coffee in sealed filters brews in cold water overnight, yielding a strong, smooth coffee that requires less ice when consumed. Happily, cold brewing is 100% feasible to do at home, as I've laid out in the DIY guide below. You'll save money, avoid using heat and electricity, and best of all, wind up with a cup—or pitcher—of delicious cold coffee that will satisfy your inner coffee snob.

Note: If you're pulling an all-nighter or gearing up for an early morning triathlon, the espresso powder–infused Jolt ice cubes (page 208) will provide an extra, dilution-free shot of cold octane.

While the cold-brew method is simple, many choices are involved (type of coffee, grind, filter, brewing duration, etc.)—so I've turned to the experts at Tandem Coffee + Bakery, purveyors of the best cup o' cold joe in Portland, for tips and best practices. Granted, Tandem typically makes twenty quarts at a time, but the principles they espouse remain valid whatever your desired volume.

COFFEE

Juicier, higher-acidity coffees, such as Ethiopian

GRIND

Not as fine as espresso, but finer than drip

FILTER TYPE

Large, disposable filters (Tandem recommends Toddy filters, available online)

WATER TO COFFEE RATIO

11:1 water to coffee (a gram scale is key)

BREW PROCESS

"First we pour some filtered water on the grounds in the filter just to wet them. Then we add more water and stir with a large spoon to immerse the filter. We then add the rest of the water around the filter and let it sit at room temperature overnight, for at least twelve hours. Next day, we remove the filter with the wet grounds and the cold brew is good to go!"

In short, with no fancy device needed other than specialized filters (available online or at coffee specialty stores), you are good to go. I have simplified things even further with the one quart recipe below.

MAKES 1 QUART COLD-BREW COFFEE

ACTIVE TIME: 5 MINUTES

TOTAL TIME: 12 HOURS

1 large disposable cold-brew filter bag

3 ounces finely ground coffee (between espresso grind and regular drip coffee grind), about 1⅔ cups in volume

1 quart (32 ounces) filtered water

Fill the filter bag with the coffee grounds and place in a 2-quart container. With the filter bag open and upright, carefully pour a little of the water over the grounds to wet them, making sure the ground coffee remains within the filter bag.

Tie or seal the filter bag, making sure that the sealed end is facing up, away from the water. Gently pour the rest of the water in over the coffee grounds.

Cover the top of the container loosely with a cloth and let sit out all day or overnight, about 12 hours total.

Remove the filter bag from the coffee. Serve the coffee over ice. Any remaining cold brew can be stored in the fridge. For optimal results, drink within 2 days.

SMALL
PLATES
AND
SNACKS

MULTICOLORED RAW ENERGY BITES

MAKES 40 BITES | ACTIVE TIME: 20 MINUTES | TOTAL TIME: 20 MINUTES

Not only do these bite-sized snacks offer a superlative blend of sweet, salty, and rich—they're also naturally colorful, genuinely healthy, and require no cooking whatsoever. You're welcome! The premise is to make an easy base dough packed with nutrient-rich flax, chia, and hemp seeds, then mix in different powders made primarily from pulverized freeze-dried fruit, each with its own bright color and flavor: red (strawberry or raspberry), blue (blueberry), yellow (mango-turmeric), and green (spirulina). Choose a favorite or experiment with your own for healthy, energy-rich snacks perfect for packed lunches, gym bags, or long hikes.

1 cup freeze-dried strawberries or raspberries

1 cup freeze-dried blueberries

1 cup freeze-dried mango

¼ teaspoon ground turmeric

1 tablespoon plus 1 teaspoon spirulina powder

1 cup rolled oats

½ cup oat bran

½ cup almond flour

1 tablespoon flax seeds

1 tablespoon chia seeds

1 tablespoon hemp seeds

½ cup smooth almond butter

½ cup honey

1 teaspoon pure vanilla extract

¾ teaspoon sea salt

Get your colors ready: Place the strawberries or raspberries in the bowl of a food processor and process until a powder forms, about 1 minute. Reserve 1 tablespoon powder and transfer the rest to a small bowl. Clean out the bowl of the food processor.

Repeat step 1 using the blueberries.

Combine the mangos and turmeric in the bowl of the food processor and repeat step 1.

Reserve 1 teaspoon of spirulina powder in a small bowl and place the remaining powder in a separate small bowl.

Place the oats, oat bran, almond flour, flax seeds, chia seeds, and hemp seeds in the bowl of the food processor and process until finely ground, about 1 minute.

Add the almond butter, honey, vanilla, and sea salt and process until a thick dough forms, 1 to 2 minutes.

Divide the dough into 4 equal pieces. Knead each colored powder into one of the 4 pieces to incorporate—you should end up with 4 large pieces, 1 red, 1 blue, 1 green, 1 yellow. From each piece break off tablespoon-sized chunks and roll with your hands into 1-inch balls, placing them on a plate, until all the dough is used up. Sprinkle a little of the reserved powder over each bite of like color. The bites will last about 1 week refrigerated in an airtight container.

SPICY GRILLED EGGPLANT ROMESCO DIP

MAKES ABOUT 4 CUPS | ACTIVE TIME: 30 MINUTES | TOTAL TIME: 30 MINUTES

The origins of this recipe can be traced back to Catalonia, northern Spain, where, hundreds of years ago, fishermen livened up their seafood with a saucy blend of ground almonds, garlic, peppers, tomatoes, and olive oil (and sometimes stale bread, to boot). If you recognized this as romesco sauce, you get a gold star. Here I've used grilled eggplant and sweet red onion to thicken and transform the classic romesco into a hearty dip. Served with crisp cold crunchy vegetables such as green beans, Romanesco, radicchio, and radishes and some olive oil grilled toast, the result is a light but satisfying summer meal. What's more, because it can safely sit out at room temp for a few hours, it makes a great al fresco option. It also works wonders as a sandwich spread, as part of a tinned seafood spread (see page 120), or served alongside rotisserie chicken (see page 147).

1 red bell pepper

2 tablespoons plus ½ cup extra virgin olive oil

1 small eggplant (about 12 ounces), peeled and sliced into ½-inch-thick rounds

1 medium red onion (about 12 ounces), peeled and sliced into 1-inch-thick rounds

1 Fresno or jalapeño chile

½ cup Marcona almonds

½ cup sun-dried tomatoes

1 clove garlic, smashed with the side of a chef's knife and peeled

2 tablespoons sherry vinegar

Sea salt

Freshly ground black pepper

Fresh herbs for garnish

Crunchy vegetables, such as carrots, green beans, endive, radicchio, radishes, cauliflower, broccoli, and Romanesco, for serving

Grilled bread, pita bread, or flatbread drizzled with olive oil for serving

Place the bell pepper directly on the open flame of a grill or on top of a gas burner over high heat. Use tongs to turn the bell pepper every now and then until it is completely charred, 8 to 10 minutes total. Transfer the bell pepper to a bowl and cover with foil or plastic wrap to steam, about 10 minutes. Peel and seed the bell pepper and set aside.

Meanwhile, heat a grill or grill pan to medium-high heat. Drizzle 2 tablespoons olive oil all over the eggplant, red onion, and chile. Place the vegetables on the grill, in batches if necessary, and grill until cooked through and dark grill marks form, about 10 minutes per batch. Remove from the grill, let cool slightly, peel the chile skin, and roughly chop all the vegetables. Set aside.

Place the almonds, tomatoes, and garlic in a high-powered blender or food processor and process, scraping down the sides as needed, until finely chopped, about 1 minute.

Add the vegetables, the remaining ½ cup olive oil, and the vinegar to the nut mixture and process until smooth. Season with salt and pepper. Serve with crudités and grilled bread, warmed pita, or flatbread drizzled with olive oil. Refrigerate any remaining dip in an airtight container for up to 1 week.

HOW TO SHUCK OYSTERS

To my way of thinking, there isn't much that beats a plate of cold, fresh, briny oysters on a hot day. There's a downside, though, as my fellow oyster lovers will attest. At $3 a pop at most restaurants, satisfying your oyster fix can be an expensive proposition, especially considering the relatively skimpy amount of food they provide.

There's a pearl lining here, though: a primary reason for the oyster's hefty price tag is the labor involved in preparation, so if you're game, mastering the art of shucking will pay dividends over time. Just be aware there's an accompanying risk, one roughly comparable to becoming, say, a master margarita maker. Namely, once word gets out, you may find yourself in constant demand, fielding recurring requests—in short, relegated to the position of the default supplier within your social circle. Accordingly, to some extent you may want to keep a shell—I mean a lid—on your newfound shucking skills and remain a surreptitious shucker. Just follow the instructions below, and whether openly or secretly, you'll master oyster shucking in no time.

BRING TOOLS

You'll need a) an oyster knife and b) a dishcloth and/or protective glove. Any reputable kitchen supply store or seafood market will carry oyster knives.

SUIT UP

Fold the cloth over itself in thirds to make it thick. If you have a glove, now is the time to put it on. Then wrap the dishcloth around your hand, covering both your hand and your thumb.

GET A GRIP

Place the oyster on a cutting board with the hinge end at an angle away from your hand. Grip the posterior part of the shell with your cloth-covered hand to hold it in place. The flat side should be at the top and the rounded side at the bottom.

DO THE TWIST

Exerting gentle but steady force, insert the point of the oyster knife into the hinge. Wiggle a bit to establish a steady point of contact. Holding the knife firmly, turn your wrist to twist the knife and pop open the hinge.

TOP IT OFF

Run the knife along the underside of the top shell to detach it from the oyster. Remove the top shell, taking care not to spill the liquid from the bottom shell containing the oyster.

SET IT FREE

Gently slide the knife around and under the oyster to release it from the bottom shell.

DRESS FOR SUCCESS

Arrange prepped oysters on a plate over ice, alongside any desired toppings, such as the Cucumber Radish Mignonette (page 40), finely chopped Spicy Daikon Pickles (page 223), cocktail sauce, horseradish, and/or lemon.

SLURPEE TIME

Eat oysters.

Note: If you are more of a visual learner, an online search will yield dozens of professionally made online videos with step-by-step instructions.

BUYING AND STORING OYSTERS

Oysters can contain harmful bacteria, so care must be taken when purchasing and storing them. Here a few rules of thumb:

Purchase your oysters from a reputable fishmonger. The seafood store should smell clean, not fishy. If the smell concerns you, the seafood should as well.

– Pay attention to where the oysters originated from. They should come from locations known for breeding safe-to-eat oysters. If in doubt, ask your seafood purveyor. Oysters should be labeled with where they came from and harvest dates.

– Fresh oysters must be alive before eating them. The oyster must be able to tightly close its shell. Tap on any open oyster shells. If an oyster is no longer alive, its shell will remain open and it should be discarded. If it is alive, the shell will close; it is then safe to shuck.

– Oysters should be kept on ice and refrigerated but stored out of the water. I recommend eating them within twenty-four hours of purchase to ensure freshness. This is especially true in the warmer months.

OYSTERS WITH CUCUMBER RADISH MIGNONETTE

SERVES 4 | ACTIVE TIME: 8 MINUTES | TOTAL TIME: 8 MINUTES

Mignonette is a light and bright vinegar-based sauce—simple to whip up and perfect for accompanying oysters and any other rich and/or briny shellfish that may benefit from a hit of acid—think raw clams, poached shrimp, scallops, crab, or lobster (for more on seafood spreads, read the sidebar on page 120). Just to sweeten the pot (no pun intended) I've increased visual and textural interest here by adding crisp and cooling minced cucumber and radish. Spoon a little over your oyster and you'll be in clover—oyster clover. Bonus: Any leftover mignonette can be repurposed as a convenient salad dressing starter—simply whisk in a bit of Dijon mustard and olive oil, and there's a good chance your greens will make *Vanity Fair*'s annual best-dressed list.

1¼ cups minced unpeeled seedless cucumber

¼ cup minced radish

2 tablespoons minced shallot

½ cup unseasoned rice vinegar

¼ teaspoon sea salt

¼ teaspoon freshly ground black pepper

2 cups ice cubes

12 fresh raw oysters, shucked (for tips on shucking, see page 38)

Place the cucumber, radish, shallot, vinegar, salt, and pepper in a small bowl. Stir to combine. Refrigerate until ready to serve. The mignonette can be made up to 1 day ahead of time.

To serve, place the ice in a food processor and pulse a few times, until slightly crushed. Spread the ice out onto a large tray or oyster plate and place the oysters on top of the ice. Serve the oysters immediately with a ramekin of the mignonette sauce, a small spoon, and a few oyster forks.

SCALLOP CEVICHE WITH LIME, AVOCADO, CILANTRO, AND CHILES

SERVES 4 | ACTIVE TIME: 30 MINUTES | TOTAL TIME: 4½ HOURS

Ceviche is a cold seafood dish eaten in parts of South America, Central America, and Mexico. It involves a centuries-old preparation method by which a variety of raw seafood is cured using the acidic juices of citrus fruits, as opposed to being heated via a direct heat source such as oven, grill, or stovetop. While it marinates, the seafood slowly becomes firm and opaque, a result of the citric acid from the fruit juices causing the seafood proteins to become "denatured"—in essence, cooked (on further reflection, let's just go with the latter word). In this ceviche recipe, I've paired fresh sea scallops with lime juice, red onion, avocado, cilantro, and, for kicks, spicy chiles. If the mood strikes you, serve with tortilla or pita chips for easy scooping.

1 pound dry sea scallops, with side muscles removed, cut into ½-inch pieces

¼ cup thinly sliced red onion

½ to 1 Fresno or jalapeño chile, stem removed and thinly sliced

1 cup fresh lime juice

2 tablespoons extra virgin olive oil

1 ripe avocado, peeled, pitted, and chopped

1 lime, peeled and segmented

1 cup fresh cilantro leaves with tender stems, plus more (optional) for garnish

Sea salt

Freshly ground black pepper

Place the scallops, onion, chile, and lime juice in a medium nonreactive bowl. Stir, cover, and refrigerate until the scallops are opaque and "cooked," about 4 hours.

Remove from the refrigerator and use a fine-mesh strainer to drain the scallops and discard any juices. Transfer back to the bowl and gently stir in the olive oil, avocado, lime segments, and cilantro. Season with salt and pepper. Divide among glasses or small bowls and garnish with cilantro, if desired. Serve immediately.

ROOM-TEMPERATURE HARICOTS VERTS WITH SESAME AND TRUFFLE

SERVES 4 | ACTIVE TIME: 10 MINUTES | TOTAL TIME: 20 MINUTES

Think of this recipe as an all-expenses-paid trip to Tokyo by way of Paris, in the form of a green bean. Or, to be more precise, an *haricot vert*—the elegantly thin, tender cousin of the green bean. I love the texture and sweetness of haricots verts. As for the Japanese influence, I'm topping the haricots verts with my own loosely based version of *furikake*, a popular condiment and dried topping in many Japanese dishes made from sesame seeds, seaweed, sometimes dried fish, dried egg, and chiles. My simplified adaptation uses ground, toasted sesame seeds, truffle salt, and Aleppo chile. The umami from the truffle elevates these haricots verts, in my opinion, from simple side dish to full-fledged appetizer. For me the beans are best served at room temperature, but they're also tasty refrigerated and served very cold. They can withstand the heat and won't wilt, making them a perfect addition to any outdoor meal or picnic.

1 tablespoon sea salt

1 pound haricots verts, stem ends trimmed

3 tablespoons black truffle oil

⅓ cup sesame seeds

½ teaspoon truffle salt

½ teaspoon Aleppo chile flakes

¼ teaspoon freshly ground black pepper

Combine 2 cups water and the sea salt in a medium saucepan. Bring to a boil over high heat, about 4 minutes. Add the haricots verts, using tongs to toss in the hot water until submerged, then cover with a lid and cook until the haricots verts are tender, about 6 minutes. Transfer to a large bowl of ice water to cool completely.

Drain well and transfer to a medium bowl. Toss the haricots verts with the truffle oil. Refrigerate until ready to serve.

Put the sesame seeds in a small skillet and turn the heat to medium. Cook, stirring constantly, until golden and lightly toasted, 6 to 8 minutes. Transfer to the bowl of a mortar and pestle and grind coarsely, then transfer to a small bowl. Alternatively, you can place the sesame seeds on a cutting board and use a meat mallet to crush them slightly, then transfer them to the bowl.

Stir in the truffle salt, Aleppo chile, and black pepper.

To serve, place the haricots verts on a serving platter or on 4 small plates. Top with the sesame seed mixture. Serve immediately or within a few hours.

TONNO CRUDO WITH OLIVES, LEMON, AND OLIVE OIL

SERVES 4 | ACTIVE TIME: 15 MINUTES | TOTAL TIME: 15 MINUTES

Think of this dish as Italian sashimi; crudo in Italian simply means "raw." In this recipe, fresh, uncooked tuna (tonno) is simply sliced thin and drizzled with high-quality olive oil, olives, herbs, red chile flakes, salt, and pepper. I incorporate Quick and Spicy Mediterranean Lemon Pickles (page 217) here as well—both the peel and the brine, which adds a sharp, citrus-y flavor that accentuates the fish beautifully. Raw seafood gets top billing here, so make sure you buy your tuna from a reputable fishmonger and confirm that it's sashimi grade, which means graded highly enough to eat raw. It may sound obvious, but it still bears saying: the better quality and the more in-season your ingredients are, the better your end product will be.

8 ounces sashimi-grade tuna

3 tablespoons brine from Quick and Spicy Mediterranean Lemon Pickles (page 217)

3 tablespoons extra virgin olive oil

1 teaspoon crushed red chile flakes

¼ cup finely diced peel from Quick and Spicy Mediterranean Lemon Pickles (page 217)

¼ cup pitted and sliced Castelvetrano or other green olives

2 tablespoons finely chopped fresh flat-leaf parsley

Parsley flowers and/or microgreens for garnish

Use a very sharp knife to slice the tuna into very thin slices across the grain, 1/16 to 1/8 inch thick, and place on a serving platter.

Drizzle with the lemon pickle brine, olive oil, and chile flakes.

Scatter the lemon pickle and olives over the top and sprinkle with the chopped parsley. Garnish with parsley flowers and/or microgreens. Serve immediately.

LOBSTER, ASPARAGUS, AND DAIKON SUMMER ROLLS WITH ORANGE, SESAME, AND CHILE DIPPING SAUCE

MAKES 8 ROLLS + ABOUT ⅓ CUP SAUCE | ACTIVE TIME: 25 MINUTES | TOTAL TIME: 25 MINUTES

I sometimes get asked about the difference between spring rolls and summer rolls. Both are tightly wrapped bundles often served with dipping sauces, of course, but after that things get a bit subjective and murky . . . especially with regards to spring rolls, of which there are innumerable versions. Spring rolls tend to have a crispy wrapper, often with flour and egg in the dough, and are usually (but not always) fried. They may contain cooked cellophane noodles and veggies if Southeast Asian, or shredded carrots and cabbage (and sometimes meat) if Chinese—similar to an egg roll but smaller. As for summer rolls, I think of them as primarily Vietnamese or Thai—typically soft, steamed rice wrappers containing shredded or julienned fresh veggies (raw or lightly cooked to retain their crunch) plus some form of precooked meat or seafood. That's a fair description of the recipe below (this being a hot weather cookbook, I naturally had to go summer, roll-wise).

One of my favorite go-to snacks when I want to feel satiated but not too full, summer rolls are relatively easy to make once you have the ingredients ready to go. The softened rice wrappers are the key—besides the satisfying chew they give, their neutral flavor allows the maker/filler to get creative. While shrimp are commonly found in summer rolls (and would make for a viable alternative option for this recipe, as would any shellfish native to your region), I live in Maine, so I've gone with lobster here. To balance out the richness I've added crunchy cold daikon, chewy noodles, and slightly sweet asparagus. Dunk one into the dipping sauce, which incorporates notes of orange and spicy sambal chili sauce, and you're in for a wonderful exotic treat. You can find rice wrappers, rice vermicelli, and sambal chili in your local Asian market or Asian section of your local supermarket. One small caveat: I recommend eating these right after you make them, because the rice wrapper can soggify—I believe that's the correct culinary term—if one waits too long.

recipe continues on page 48

For the dipping sauce

1 teaspoon fresh orange zest

¼ cup fresh orange juice

2 tablespoons low-sodium soy sauce

1 tablespoon toasted sesame oil

1 teaspoon sugar

1 to 2 teaspoons sambal chili sauce

For the summer rolls

3 ounces dried thin rice vermicelli

Sea salt

1 pound asparagus, bottom ends trimmed, each cut in half lengthwise if thick

8 large round rice wrappers, about 10 inches in diameter

8 ounces fresh shelled lobster meat

2 cups julienned daikon (from one 1-pound white or purple daikon using a serrated vegetable peeler)

Pickled Ginger (page 222) for serving (optional)

To make the dipping sauce

In a small bowl, whisk together the orange zest, orange juice, soy sauce, sesame oil, sugar, and chili sauce and set aside until ready to use.

To make the summer rolls

Cook the vermicelli according to the package instructions. Transfer to a bowl of ice water to stop the cooking, then drain and set aside. Reserve the bowl of ice water for the asparagus.

Fill a large high-sided skillet with 1 inch of water. Bring to a boil over high heat, about 4 minutes. Heavily salt the water and add the asparagus. Cook until the asparagus is crisp-tender, about 3 minutes, then use tongs to transfer to the bowl of ice water to stop the cooking. Drain the asparagus and set aside until ready to use.

Fill a large shallow dish with very hot water. Working quickly, completely submerge one rice wrapper in the hot water until soft and pliable, 10 to 15 seconds.

Remove from the water and place on a cutting board. Lay 1 ounce lobster meat in the center of the rice wrapper along with some of the vermicelli, daikon, and asparagus. Fold the bottom half of the rice paper wrapper over the filling, then fold in the sides of the wrapper. Pressing down firmly, hold the folds in place and tightly roll the wrapper up from the bottom to the top, then transfer to a large platter. Repeat with the remaining rice wrappers and fillings. Serve the summer rolls immediately, with the dipping sauce and pickled ginger, if desired.

COLD TOFU IN DASHI WITH RADISH, SCALLIONS, SESAME, AND BONITO

SERVES 4 | ACTIVE TIME: 15 MINUTES | TOTAL TIME: 1 HOUR 25 MINUTES

I became acquainted with this delightful dish years ago during a summer abroad in Japan. It turned out to be one of those foods that seems simple and mild at first taste, but gains interest with each bite as the subtle and complex flavors emerge. Commonly served as a late afternoon snack or even as part of a breakfast, it's built around a foundation of homemade *dashi*, a smoky and savory broth that serves as the base of many a Japanese dish (including, notably, miso soup). With its flavor derived from *kombu* (a type of large, thick edible seaweed) and bonito (dried, fermented, smoked tuna flakes), the dashi serves here as a rich umami bath for your tofu to chillax in, along with a variety of flavorful toppings: grated ginger, mildly spicy grated daikon, bright and flavorful scallions, robust sesame seeds, and more flaky and smoky *bonito*. For the tofu, I've chosen the silken variety to employ its spoonable, custard-like texture. Serve as a solo snack or side dish to any Japanese-themed meal.

½ ounce dried kombu seaweed pieces

1 cup water

¾ cup loosely packed katsuobushi (dried bonito flakes), plus ¼ cup more for topping

3 tablespoons mirin

2 tablespoons soy sauce

1 pound silken tofu, cut into 4 equal pieces

2 tablespoons toasted sesame oil

¼ cup grated peeled daikon

¼ cup thinly sliced scallions

2 tablespoons grated fresh ginger

1 tablespoon toasted sesame seeds

Combine the kombu and water in a small saucepan. Bring to a simmer over medium heat, 6 to 8 minutes.

With the heat off, add the ¾ cup bonito and let steep for 10 minutes. Strain through a fine-mesh strainer into a large measuring cup, discarding the kombu and bonito. Stir in the mirin and soy sauce, then refrigerate until cold, about 1 hour.

Place the tofu in 4 small shallow bowls. Pour the broth in roughly equal amounts over each of the squares of tofu, then drizzle on the sesame oil. Over the top of each piece of tofu, sprinkle grated daikon, scallions, ginger, sesame seeds, and the remaining ¼ cup bonito flakes. Serve immediately.

ONIGIRI WITH SESAME SALMON

MAKES ABOUT 9 ONIGIRI | ACTIVE TIME: 50 MINUTES | TOTAL TIME: 1 HOUR 15 MINUTES

I first tried onigiri—Japanese rice balls filled with various savory fillings—at a friend's house when I was a kid. Later, as a teenager, I spent a summer teaching English in Japan, and they became my go-to staple—a familiar comfort food in a strange land. You can find onigiri in many Japanese markets, where they're often made fresh daily; a few onigiri make a simple, satisfying, portable, delicious, and economical lunch. Typically served room temperature, onigiri come in all shapes and sizes, but perhaps most often—as in this recipe—are found in a triangular shape with a rectangle of crunchy, toasted nori seaweed folded around one end. A few things to keep in mind: First, if the salmon filling on its own tastes quite salty, it's meant to. Onigiri fillings are generally salty and intense in order to give the rice, which doesn't have much flavor in and of itself, a boost. Second, if you have trouble forming your onigiri into a perfect equilateral shape, have no fear— rolled into a ball, they're just as tasty and still attractive. The onigiri can be stuffed and shaped, placed in an airtight container, and refrigerated up to a couple hours ahead of time. Finally, proximity to moisture can make seaweed quickly go from crisp to limp, so consider waiting to affix the seaweed to your onigiri until just before eating.

2 cups sushi rice

4 ounces center-cut boneless, skinless salmon fillet

Sea salt

1 tablespoon canola oil

2 teaspoons toasted sesame oil

1 tablespoon toasted sesame seeds, divided

2 (8 by 7½-inch) rectangles toasted nori

Rinse the sushi rice in a fine-mesh strainer under cold water until the water runs clear. Cook the sushi rice according to package directions (I use 2 cups rice to 3 cups water). Transfer the rice to a large bowl, mixing gently with a spoon intermittently to help release the heat, until the rice cools enough to handle, 20 to 30 minutes.

Meanwhile, pat the salmon dry with paper towels and season all over with ½ teaspoon salt. Heat the canola oil in a medium cast-iron or nonstick skillet over medium heat. Add the salmon and cook until a golden crust forms on the surface, 2 to 3 minutes. Use a fish spatula to carefully flip the salmon over and cook until cooked through, about 3 more minutes. Transfer to a cutting board to rest, about 5 minutes, then roughly chop the salmon and place in a medium bowl.

Stir in the sesame oil, 1½ teaspoons of the sesame seeds, and ¼ teaspoon salt until combined. Set aside. This can be done up to 1 day ahead of time and kept refrigerated in an airtight container.

Fill a medium bowl with 2 cups water. Add 2 teaspoons salt to the water and stir to combine.

Use kitchen shears to cut each nori sheet into 8 (3½ by 2-inch) rectangles. You will need 9 total. Save the extra nori to use in a recipe such as the Tamago with Rice, Sesame Seeds, and Pickled Plum on page 22. Set aside.

Dampen your hands in the saltwater. Take a heaping ⅓ cup rice out of the bowl and place on a clean cutting board. Use dampened hands to form into a 3-inch triangle that is about 1 inch thick on the surface of the cutting board. The corners of the triangle should be rounded, not sharp.

Use your finger to make an indentation into the center of the triangle. Fill the hole with about 2 teaspoons salmon mixture. Cover with a bit more rice.

Repeat the above steps with the remaining rice and salmon mixture to make 8 more onigiri (9 in all).

Prior to serving, wrap a nori rectangle around the bottom of each triangle. Sprinkle each onigiri with sesame seeds and serve immediately.

VARIATIONS ON A DEVILED EGG

Premade, portable, and served cold, deviled eggs make great hot-weather comfort food. On Sundays, I whip up a large batch to keep for snacks, breakfast, or lunch addition during the busy week ahead. They are also quite versatile and easy to personalize according to mood, sudden inspiration, or whatever you're out of that day.

CLASSIC

For 12 deviled eggs, place 6 large eggs in a medium saucepan, cover with water by 1 inch, bring to a boil over high heat, immediately cover, turn off the heat, and let the eggs steam for 9 to 11 minutes.

Drain and run the eggs under cold water until cool enough to handle. Return the eggs to the empty saucepan and, carefully, swirl the pan enough to knock the eggs around and crack the shells all over. Transfer to a large bowl of ice water and let chill for 10 minutes. Once chilled, peel the eggs *in the bowl of ice water*. Stay the course, numb fingers and all (it's hot out, right?), and you'll have perfectly peeled eggs without craters or tears.

Halve the peeled eggs and scoop the yolks out into a medium bowl. Set the white halves aside on a serving platter.

Using a whisk, tap the yolks apart, then whisk until finely ground. Stir in ⅓ cup mayonnaise or aioli, 2 teaspoons mustard of choice, and a pinch of hot chile powder (Aleppo, cayenne, hot paprika, etc.) or dash of hot sauce; season with salt and pepper.

Pipe or spoon the deviled mixture back into the white halves, then garnish as desired.

RED DEVIL

Stir smoked paprika into the yolk mixture and drizzle finished deviled eggs with adobo sauce.

SEA-DEVIL

Top finished deviled eggs with chilled crabmeat, lobster, or shrimp.

GREEN EGGS AND HERBS

Stir a bit of mashed avocado into the yolk mixture and top finished deviled eggs with chopped fresh chives or parsley.

KOREAN-INSPIRED SOFT-BOILED EGGS

Similar to deviled eggs, but with a few key differences: The eggs are soft-boiled, not hard-boiled; and, instead of the yolks getting scooped and mashed, the soft yolks stay put and get drizzled, sprinkled, and topped with various condiments.

For these, follow the classic method but steam eggs only 3 to 4 minutes, then chill and peel the eggs in the ice water, as directed. Slice the eggs in half, drizzle with 2 tablespoons toasted sesame oil, and sprinkle with 1 tablespoon toasted sesame seeds. Season with Korean red pepper flakes, then top each with kimchi and thinly sliced scallions.

SALADS

BLUSHING FRUIT SALAD

SERVES 4 | ACTIVE TIME: 20 MINUTES | TOTAL TIME: 30 MINUTES

Coming to terms with the reality that I always go for the pink, red, and purple fruit in fruit salad was what led me to this recipe. There may be some connection here to my daughter's refusal to drink any smoothie that isn't white (see Mock Vanilla Milkshake, page 12). Apparently, we are a visually driven household. But in full disclosure, I've never been particularly fond of the classic, mainstream fruit salad. Nothing against melon and pineapple, but the precut polyhedrons seen in cafeterias and takeout refrigerators across the nation tend to be prepped way in advance, with less-than-ripe fruit used intentionally to extend shelf life. Accordingly, at (say) a brunch or buffet, I'll generally take a pass, except for a couple of berries (not all of them of course; that would be like the time my freshman year roommate dug every last chocolate chunk out a pint of Ben and Jerry's with a fork—not that I'm still bitter about it more than twenty years later . . .).

Anyhow, to double down on my red-purple-pink theme, I've added some less standard fruits (figs, pomegranate, pluots) as well as incorporated Middle Eastern flavors such as rosewater (see Red Grapefruit–Rose Sorbet, page 165) and sumac. The latter—a spice that comes from dried and crushed sumac berries—livens up any dish, thanks to its lovely red color and tart flavor. The overall result, I think you will find, is a fragrant bowlful with a lack of resemblance to run-of-the mill fruit salad that will leave your guests gazing at you with grateful "Why didn't anyone else think of that?" expressions. Just remember that freshness is key, and it's one of the main reasons you're going to all this effort—so pick out the best-looking, ripest seasonal fruit and cut it yourself.

2 cups (1-inch) cubes seedless watermelon

2 cups cherries, stems removed, halved, and pitted

1 cup hulled and halved (quartered if large) strawberries

1 cup raspberries

4 fresh black figs, quartered

2 plumcots or pluots, halved, pitted, and cut into 1-inch pieces

1 cup pomegranate seeds

5 tablespoons sugar

2 to 4 tablespoons rosewater

Ground sumac for sprinkling

Flaky salt for sprinkling

Place the watermelon, cherries, strawberries, raspberries, figs, plumcots or pluots, and pomegranate seeds in a large bowl.

In a small bowl, whisk together the sugar and rosewater until the sugar dissolves. Pour the rosewater syrup over the fruit and gently toss to coat. Let macerate in the rosewater syrup for at least 10 minutes or up to 1 hour. The longer the fruit macerates, the more flavor it will take on.

Serve the fruit salad in bowls or on plates sprinkled with sumac and flaky salt. The fruit salad can be stored in an airtight container in the refrigerator for up to 2 days (garnish just before serving).

MATCHSTICK APPLE, JICAMA, AND FENNEL SLAW WITH HONEY LEMON VINAIGRETTE

SERVES 4 AS AN ENTREE OR 8 AS A SIDE SALAD | ACTIVE TIME: 25 MINUTES | TOTAL TIME: 25 MINUTES

This sweet, salty, crunchy salad is a refreshing option to make for a picnic or bring to a cookout, anywhere food may be in transit or sitting out in the sun for a while—the apple, jicama, and fennel retain their crunch and the citrus in the dressing prevents the apples from turning brown. In other words, it probably withstands hot conditions better than you and I would. If you have leftovers, save them; the slaw's crunch and flavor make a superb supplement to a sliced turkey or ham sandwich.

1 tablespoon fresh lemon zest

3 tablespoons fresh lemon juice

3 tablespoons honey

2 tablespoons Dijon mustard

⅓ cup extra virgin olive oil

Sea salt

Freshly ground black pepper

1 sweet apple, such as Pink Lady or Gala

1 Granny Smith apple

1 fennel bulb, bottom trimmed, cored, and thinly sliced

2 cups peeled and julienned jicama

2 medium heads purple or green endive, thinly sliced

1 cup fennel fronds, coarsely chopped

1 cup fresh flat-leaf parsley leaves

6 peppadew peppers, coarsely chopped

½ cup toasted salted sunflower seeds, plus more for garnish

Place the lemon zest, lemon juice, honey, and mustard in the bottom of a large bowl and whisk to combine. Slowly drizzle in the olive oil until incorporated. Season with salt and pepper.

Use a knife or mandoline to julienne the apples. Discard the cores. Top the dressing with the apples and toss to coat so that they don't start oxidizing and turn brown.

Add the fennel, jicama, endive, fennel fronds, parsley, peppadew peppers, and sunflower seeds. Toss to combine. Sprinkle with the remaining sunflower seeds and serve immediately, or refrigerate for up to 1 day (garnish just before serving).

RECEPTORS:
DOES EATING SOMETHING HOT
ACTUALLY COOL A PERSON DOWN?

It has been frequently observed that inhabitants of hot and humid environments worldwide—regional examples include Asia, Africa, Mexico, Central and South America, the southern United States, and the Caribbean, among others—incorporate spicy foods into their regular diets and/or drink hot tea to cool down their body temperatures. To better understand this phenomenon, some elementary bioscience is helpful. It seems there are special protein structures called receptors in our mouths that exchange signals with our nervous systems. One of these is called the TRPV1 receptor (aka the "capsaicin receptor"), and it is specially designed to detect food that is hot, either spice-wise or temperature-wise. When triggered, the TRPV1 receptor cues the nervous system to transmit a signal to the hypothalamus—our brain's thermostat, as it were—notifying it that it's time to turn on the body's primary internal AC mechanism: in other words, to sweat.

Sweating, as you may know, allows the body to release heat in order to cool off, assuming the sweat can evaporate (thus this approach works better in dry heat than humidity). Many nutritionists believe that the sweating caused by eating spicy food ultimately cools your body better and longer than eating cold food— and conversely, that eating cold food can sometimes have the opposite effect. According to this school of thought, cold food may cool the body temporarily (at least those parts of the body it comes into contact with), but the effect is short lived. Once digestion occurs— especially if the food is rich and fatty (think ice cream)—the feeling of being overheated

can become exacerbated, not relieved. That's why the recipes that are served cold in this book tend to be on the lighter side, and I recommend eating a smaller serving of those with a high fat content.

For examples of "heat to cool" in this book, see Sweet Lemongrass-Ginger Tea (page 193), Frisée with Crispy Olive Oil–Fried Egg and Harissa Oil (page 27), Spicy Papaya Slaw (page 61), and Spicy Daikon Pickles (page 223).

For the sake of completeness, I'll mention a few additional theories I came across in my research as to why spicy food may be more prevalent in hot climes across the globe. One is simply that many spicy foods (chiles chief among them) grow best in hot weather, and locals naturally tend to eat and cook with whatever is native to their region. Others assert that spices are used in hot climates mainly because of their antibacterial properties. Heat makes food spoil faster, and spices help to preserve it; therefore, in this view, in many hot climate regions, spice was used to extend the shelf life of food (or, frankly, to mask its less-than-fresh flavor), and presumably the spice became a traditional part of those cuisines over the centuries. Another line of thought: heavily spiced foods may be common in places where hunger was more prevalent due to poverty, such as India, because many spices— chile pepper, for example—serve as an appetite suppressant.

SPICY PAPAYA SLAW

SERVES 4 TO 8 | ACTIVE TIME: 20 MINUTES | TOTAL TIME: 20 MINUTES

This refreshing salad makes use of the tropical, mildly sweet, and often-overlooked papaya. As you can probably tell, I have strong opinions about this unsung hero of a fruit (for more, see page 17)—no doubt that's why I've given the papaya star billing in this recipe, surrounded with a versatile cast of supporting players, including crunchy red cabbage, cilantro, and chiles. This lovable, ragtag crew proceeds to get entangled in a series of misadventures, such as being tossed in a sweet, spicy, salty, and tart dressing. Critics nationwide are calling the result "a feel-good summer slaw surprise for the whole family."

Achieving blockbuster status takes the right texture from the start. To achieve the desired julienne cut, I recommend using a serrated vegetable peeler, one of my favorite kitchen tools. (You can achieve good results with a spiralizer as well.) This slaw makes a great little side on its own, and also can be used as a condiment to cut through the richness of roasted or barbecued meats—it's a key component, for example, of the Pan-Seared Pork Sandwich with Spicy Papaya Slaw and Spicy Pepper Jelly on Sourdough (page 115).

4 cups julienned, firm but ripe papaya (first peeled and seeded using a serrated vegetable peeler)

4 cups shredded red cabbage (from 1 medium cabbage)

2 cups fresh cilantro leaves and sprigs

1 jalapeño chile, stem removed and finely chopped

1 clove garlic, peeled and finely chopped

¼ cup fresh lime juice

¼ cup low-sodium soy sauce or low-sodium tamari (see note)

1 tablespoon honey

2 tablespoons canola oil

Sea salt (optional)

Freshly ground black pepper (optional)

Place the papaya, cabbage, and cilantro in a large serving bowl.

In a small bowl, whisk together the jalapeño, garlic, lime juice, soy sauce, honey, and canola oil.

Pour the dressing over the slaw mixture and gently toss to combine. Season with salt and pepper, if desired. Serve immediately or within a few hours.

Note: Regular soy sauce has its place, as does low-sodium soy sauce. Opting for low-sodium soy sauce as an ingredient gives you more control over flavor and salt content. Here, I wanted lots of deep-umami soy flavor but less salt. Anyone can then add sea salt to taste to each individual portion without risk of over-seasoning the whole salad.

FRESH CORN SALAD WITH PEAS AND HERBS

SERVES 4 | ACTIVE TIME: 25 MINUTES | TOTAL TIME: 25 MINUTES

Consisting of fresh green pea puree topped with crunchy and flavorful corn, peas, pea tendrils, radicchio, and herbs, dressed in oil and grainy mustard and topped with crumbled ricotta salata cheese, this salad is creamy, cool, crunchy, salty, sweet, and fresh-tasting all at once—a sort of concentrated dose of summertime. Thanks to its crisp textures and summery flavors, it makes a super accompaniment to grilled steak, chicken, sausage, or seafood, and it tends to go over like gangbusters at a barbecue—just brace yourself for enthusiastic praise and recipe requests.

For the pea puree

2 cups shelled or frozen and thawed peas

½ cup water

1 tablespoon fresh lemon zest

1 tablespoon fresh lemon juice

1 tablespoon sugar

¼ cup extra virgin olive oil

½ teaspoon sea salt

½ teaspoon freshly ground black pepper

For the dressing

2 tablespoons grainy mustard

1 tablespoon white wine vinegar

½ teaspoon sugar

¼ teaspoon sea salt

½ teaspoon freshly ground black pepper

¼ cup extra virgin olive oil

For the salad

2 cups raw corn kernels (from 2 to 3 corn cobs)

2 cups sugar snap peas, sliced in half lengthwise

2 cups pea tendrils

1 cup thinly sliced radicchio

½ cup coarsely chopped fresh herbs, such as dill, mint, and flat-leaf parsley

1 cup crumbled ricotta salata cheese

Edible flowers (optional), such as borage, marigold, or radish flowers, for garnish

To make the pea puree
Place the shelled peas, water, lemon zest, lemon juice, sugar, olive oil, salt, and pepper in a food processor or blender and process until smooth. The puree can be made a day ahead of time, if desired. Divide the pea puree among 4 large plates and smooth out with a spoon or offset spatula. Set aside.

To make the dressing
In a small bowl, whisk to combine the mustard, vinegar, sugar, salt, and pepper, then whisk in the olive oil to incorporate.

To make the salad
Divide the corn among the 4 plates with the pea puree and top with the sugar snap peas, pea tendrils, radicchio, and herbs. Drizzle with the dressing, sprinkle with the ricotta salata, and garnish with the edible flowers if desired. Serve immediately.

SHAVED SALAD IN CREAMY TAHINI DRESSING

SERVES 4 TO 6 (MAKES ABOUT ¾ CUP DRESSING) | ACTIVE TIME: 25 MINUTES | TOTAL TIME: 25 MINUTES

Technically, June 21 is the first day of summer. But for me, summer doesn't truly begin until a knock at the door signifies that a neighbor or friend has arrived to gift me their surplus zucchini—a phenomenon I have come to accept as inevitable, not unlike the phases of the moon. This salad was created explicitly to use up just such a gifted pile of zucchini in my fridge, which was in danger of being relegated to the compost bucket if it didn't receive a meaningful assignment before long. I've never been a fan of cooked zucchini, due in large part to its rather mushy texture—but raw zucchini is, to my way of thinking, underrated and underutilized; a well-kept secret. Starting with this principle, I shaved my zucchini raw, and did the same with various other inhabitants of my produce drawer; thus was born this summery, fresh, and colorful salad (thanks to which I continue to receive zucchini gladly to this day). By the way, if you suspect that a Mediterranean influence is at work here, based on the tangy, slightly sweet tahini dressing and chopped, toasted pistachio nuts, you're onto something.

Note: Because raw veggies can be a bit woody if cut too thickly, I've thinly shaved and sliced them here. This adds crunch, facilitates easy chew and digestion, and allows the salad to soak up the dressing.

For the dressing

¼ cup tahini

¼ cup extra virgin olive oil

2 tablespoons fresh lemon juice

1 teaspoon honey

1 clove garlic, peeled and finely chopped

3 to 4 tablespoons water

Sea salt

Freshly ground black pepper

For the salad

8 ounces thick asparagus spears, ends trimmed

1¼ pounds unpeeled zucchini (about 4 medium)

1 small raw beet (about 5 ounces), peeled and very thinly sliced

2 medium rainbow radishes (about 6 ounces total), stem ends trimmed, halved, and very thinly sliced

2 mini seedless cucumbers or 6 ounces seedless cucumber, thinly sliced

¾ cup roughly chopped toasted and salted shelled pistachio nuts

To make the dressing

In a medium bowl, whisk together the tahini, olive oil, lemon juice, honey, garlic, and water to desired consistency. Season with salt and pepper. Set aside.

To make the salad

Using a vegetable peeler or mandoline, carefully slice the asparagus lengthwise into long, thin strips. Place in a large bowl.

Thinly slice the zucchini lengthwise with the vegetable peeler or mandoline. When you reach the inner part with the seeds, stop peeling (you only want to use the outer layers of the zucchini; save the seedy core for another use). Add the sliced zucchini to the bowl with the asparagus, along with the beet, radishes, and cucumbers.

Divide the salad among plates. Drizzle all over with the dressing and sprinkle with the chopped pistachios. Serve immediately or within a few hours (garnish just before serving).

MIDDLE EASTERN CRUNCH SALAD

SERVES 4 TO 6 | ACTIVE TIME: 25 MINUTES | TOTAL TIME: 25 MINUTES

This vibrant salad is built around a foundation of traditional Middle Eastern spices and ingredients. Its flavors, I like to think, will transport those who eat it to the sunny Levant. In truth, if this recipe evokes anything for me, it's my Brooklyn days—specifically, the Middle Eastern restaurants and markets in Boerum Hill and adjacent neighborhoods that I used to pass on my way to work. From these establishments, mouthwatering smells of fresh pita, falafel, and shawarma invariably emanated, causing passersby to veer off-course, cross the threshold, and eventually leave encumbered with to-go bundles filled with succulent grilled kebabs, hummus, za'atar bread, muhammara sauce, and baklava.

Getting back to the salad at hand, though, this recipe consists of cold elements (crisp, crunchy vegetables and sweet, chewy dates) mixed with warm ones (crispy olive oil–fried chickpeas and pita croutons). This assemblage of elements is tossed twice—first in a flavorful spice mixture (earthy cumin, floral coriander, mildly spicy Aleppo chile, and tangy dried ground sumac), and then in a lightly sweet, salty, lemony dressing. The resulting amalgamation of flavors and textures will lift the spirits of even the most bedraggled desert traveler.

For the dressing

2 tablespoons fresh lemon juice

1 teaspoon honey

1 clove garlic, peeled and finely chopped

⅓ cup extra virgin olive oil

Sea salt

Freshly ground black pepper

For the salad

1 cup halved grape tomatoes

1 English cucumber, cut into 1-inch dice (about 2¼ cups)

1 romaine lettuce heart, chopped

2 cups baby arugula

1 large or 2 small endives, chopped (about 2 cups)

½ cup torn fresh mint leaves

1 cup chopped pitted Medjool dates

For the crunchy part

1⅓ cups chickpeas (from one 15-ounce can), rinsed and drained

2 teaspoons ground cumin

1 teaspoon ground coriander

1 teaspoon ground sumac

1 teaspoon Aleppo chile flakes

½ teaspoon sea salt

½ teaspoon freshly ground black pepper

6 tablespoons extra virgin olive oil, divided

1 medium pita bread, cut into ½-inch pieces (about 1¾ cups)

To make the dressing

In a small bowl, whisk together the lemon juice, honey, garlic, and olive oil until combined. Season with salt and pepper. Set aside.

To make the salad

Combine the tomatoes, cucumber, lettuce, arugula, endive, mint, and dates in a large bowl. Set aside.

To make the crunchy part

Lay the chickpeas out on a paper towel–lined plate. Place another paper towel over the top and pat dry as much as possible. This step will help the chickpeas to crisp when fried in the oil.

Combine the cumin, coriander, sumac, Aleppo chile, salt, and black pepper in a medium bowl. Set aside.

Heat 4 tablespoons of the olive oil in a medium saucepan over medium-high heat. When hot, stir in the chickpeas and cook, stirring a few times, until golden brown and the skins are crisp, about 8 minutes. Transfer the chickpeas back to the bowl with a slotted spoon so that some of the oil drains to the bowl with the spices.

Add the remaining 2 tablespoons olive oil and the pita to the saucepan and cook, stirring a few times, until the pita bread pieces are golden brown and crisp, 2 to 3 minutes. Transfer to the bowl with the spices and toss to coat.

Toss the salad with the dressing, then add the crunchy part and toss again to coat. Serve immediately.

SPICY CHICKPEA AND HERB SALAD OVER OLIVE OIL LABNEH

SERVES 4 | ACTIVE TIME: 20 MINUTES | TOTAL TIME: 20 MINUTES

This Mediterranean-inspired no-cook meal has a little bit of everything going on: tangy, briny, and spicy flavors and crunchy textures on top of cool, creamy labneh, a soft Middle Eastern cheese made from strained yogurt. Greek yogurt makes an easy substitute if you can't find labneh itself—sticklers can strain the yogurt through cheesecloth set over a bowl for a day or two in the refrigerator to better approximate its characteristic texture.

2 cups labneh or whole milk plain Greek yogurt

6 tablespoons extra virgin olive oil, divided

¾ teaspoon sea salt

2 (15.5-ounce) cans chickpeas, drained, rinsed, then drained again

1½ cups chopped seedless cucumber

1 large red bell pepper, stem removed, seeded, and chopped (about 1¼ cups)

⅓ cup oil-cured olives, pitted and sliced

1 cup roughly chopped fresh flat-leaf parsley leaves

1 tablespoon chopped fresh rosemary

2 tablespoons chopped preserved lemon peel from Quick and Spicy Mediterranean Lemon Pickles (page 217)

¼ cup pulp and juice from Quick and Spicy Mediterranean Lemon Pickles (page 217)

1 to 3 teaspoons finely chopped jalapeño chile, to taste

Place the labneh, 4 tablespoons of the olive oil, and the salt in a medium bowl and stir until completely smooth.

In a large bowl, combine the chickpeas, cucumber, bell pepper, olives, parsley, rosemary, lemon peel, lemon pickle juice, jalapeño, and remaining 2 tablespoons olive oil. Gently toss to combine.

Place about ½ cup labneh in the middle of each of 4 plates. Press a spoon in the middle of the mound and move out in a swiping motion to create a swirl on the plate. Top each plate with a mound of the chickpea salad. Serve immediately.

GRILLED SOURDOUGH PANZANELLA WITH HEIRLOOM TOMATOES AND HERBS

SERVES 4 | ACTIVE TIME: 15 MINUTES | TOTAL TIME: 35 MINUTES

Panzanella, an Italian rustic bread salad, is not only delicious—it's an ingenious way of using up the leftover stale ends and bits of bread and those almost-but-not-quite-overripe tomatoes that otherwise would get thrown out or composted. The classic approach is to let stale bread soften in the juices and flesh of ripe, plump tomatoes, and then add aromatics, other veggies (optional), vinegar, and a couple healthy glugs of the finest quality olive oil. The trick to a good panzanella is allotting enough time for the bread to soak up the tomato juices and dressing; all that flavor getting sopped up into the bread is where the magic lies. My version uses grilled bread because I love the flavor that the char adds. But fellow heatstroke victims need not despair—the bread takes only minutes to grill.

⅓ cup extra virgin olive oil, plus more for the grill

8 ounces sourdough bread, cut into 1-inch-thick slices

2 cloves garlic, peeled and each cut in half

3 tablespoons red wine vinegar

1 tablespoon capers in brine, drained (do not rinse)

1 teaspoon sugar

1 teaspoon sea salt

¼ teaspoon freshly ground black pepper

2¼ pounds heirloom tomatoes, coarsely chopped, reserving seeds and juices

1 cup packed fresh basil leaves, torn if large

½ cup packed fresh flat-leaf parsley leaves

Preheat a grill or grill pan to medium-high heat.

Brush oil on the grill and place slices of bread (in batches if necessary) on the grill. Cook until the bread is slightly charred and has nice grill marks on each side, 3 to 5 minutes per side.

While still hot, rub each slice of bread all over with the garlic until a subtle garlic aroma coats the toast, then set aside.

In a large bowl, whisk together the ⅓ cup olive oil, vinegar, capers, sugar, salt, and pepper.

Add the tomatoes, seeds, juices, and all to the bowl with the dressing and toss to combine.

Let cool slightly, then tear or slice the bread into 1-inch pieces and add to the bowl with the tomatoes. Gently toss everything together so the juices and flavors of the dressing begin to absorb into the crusty, charred, garlicky bread. Let it sit for about 20 minutes at room temperature to let the bread soften up and absorb the flavors. Then add the herbs and gently toss to combine. Serve immediately or within a few hours (add the herbs just before serving).

SEARED EGGPLANT WITH MINT, BASIL, AND WALNUTS IN YOGURT OLIVE OIL DRESSING

SERVES 4 | ACTIVE TIME: 25 MINUTES | TOTAL TIME: 25 MINUTES

Its glamorous and vaguely sinister-sounding name notwithstanding, the nightshade family boasts several of my favorite fruits and vegetables, including bell peppers, tomatoes, and eggplants, which hit peak ripeness during the hot and humid late summer months. Keen eggplant spotters at farmers markets during August will discover alternate colors—white, green, and orange, for example—as well as shapes and sizes that run the gamut beyond the familiar aubergine oblong. The great thing about eggplant is that its mild flavors and satisfying texture take on aspects of whatever you do to or put with it. Here, that's a delicious array of flavors, from the sweet (honey) to the sour-tangy (yogurt, mustard, vinegar), to the fragrant (herbs, garlic), to the slightly smoky (seared in a hot skillet).

¼ cup whole milk plain yogurt

3 tablespoons extra virgin olive oil, plus more for drizzling

1 tablespoon grainy mustard

1 teaspoon white wine vinegar

1 teaspoon honey

1 small clove garlic, peeled and minced

¼ teaspoon Aleppo chile flakes

Flaky sea salt

Freshly ground black pepper

4 to 5 small eggplants (about 1¾ pounds total), such as Italian, graffiti, or any variety that looks good or is in season

¾ cup raw walnut halves

½ cup fresh basil leaves, torn if large

½ cup fresh mint leaves, torn if large

In a medium bowl, whisk together the yogurt, 3 tablespoons olive oil, the mustard, vinegar, honey, garlic, and chile flakes. Season with salt and pepper and set aside.

Cut the stem ends off the eggplants and cut vertically into ¼-inch-thick slices. Set aside.

Heat a large cast-iron skillet over medium-high heat and cook the walnuts, stirring a few times, until toasted and almost charred in parts, about 4 minutes. Remove to a small bowl and set aside.

Drizzle the eggplant slices lightly with olive oil. With the heat still on medium-high, add the slices to the skillet in batches and let cook, flipping halfway through cooking, until charred in parts, 2 to 3 minutes per side. Transfer the eggplant to large plates or a serving platter and sprinkle very lightly with salt. Continue cooking the remaining eggplant, placing it on the platter, and sprinkling with salt until all the eggplant is cooked.

Drizzle the eggplant all over with the dressing. Use your hands to break and crumble the walnuts over the top. Sprinkle everywhere with the basil and mint. Serve warm or at room temperature within a few hours (garnish just before serving).

WAKAME AND CRAB SUNOMONO

SERVES 4 | ACTIVE TIME: 12 MINUTES | TOTAL TIME: 32 MINUTES

Sunomono is a cold, vinegary Japanese salad that consists, more often than not, of cucumber and some type of seafood. My version uses sweet fresh crab and includes creamy avocado to balance out the sharpness of the vinegar and *wakame*. Wakame, a type of seaweed that has been cultivated in Japan for centuries, has a fresh ocean-y flavor and chewy texture. As a Maine resident I am fortunate to have access to locally produced wakame, but you should be able to find it at most health food or Asian markets. Wakame is an excellent source of calcium, potassium, iodine, and vitamin A. Potassium-rich foods are worth seeking out when it's hot, by the way, since low potassium levels can cause fatigue and extra sensitivity to heat.

1 (12-ounce) seedless cucumber, very thinly sliced into rounds

2 teaspoons sea salt

¾ ounce dried wakame (about ⅔ cup)

¼ cup rice vinegar

2 teaspoons sugar

1 tablespoon mirin

1 tablespoon low-sodium soy sauce

1 avocado, pitted, peeled, and thinly sliced

8 ounces lump crabmeat, thoroughly picked of shell

2 teaspoons toasted sesame oil

1 teaspoon toasted sesame seeds

Place the cucumber in a medium bowl along with the salt. Use clean hands to mix the salt into the cucumber until combined. Let sit until slight softening occurs, about 10 minutes.

Meanwhile, place the wakame in a separate medium bowl and cover with 3 cups water. Let the seaweed soak until it is reconstituted, about 10 minutes.

Place the cucumber in a fine-mesh strainer and run under cold water to remove the extra salt. Drain the cucumber and return to a clean medium bowl.

Drain the wakame, then use your hands to squeeze out as much extra water as possible. Transfer the wakame to the bowl with the cucumber. Stir to combine.

In a small bowl, whisk together the vinegar, sugar, mirin, and soy sauce. Pour the dressing over the seaweed and cucumber, toss to combine, and let sit for 10 more minutes for the flavors to develop.

Divide the cucumber and wakame among 4 bowls and pour any remaining dressing over the tops of each. Top each bowl with some of the sliced avocado and crabmeat. Drizzle each salad with some of the sesame oil and sprinkle with sesame seeds. Serve immediately.

THAI CELERY SALAD WITH SHRIMP, PEANUTS, CHILES, AND CILANTRO

SERVES 4 | ACTIVE TIME: 35 MINUTES | TOTAL TIME: 1 HOUR 35 MINUTES

Understanding that both celery and peanuts are prevalent in Southeast Asian cuisines, I decided to give the classic peanut-butter-on-celery-sticks combo from childhood a sophisticated makeover inspired by hot-cold Thai salads. Both Eastern and Western medicine endorse celery for its cooling, anti-inflammatory properties, making it a natural go-to for hot-weather cooking. More important, I've always been a fan of celery personally. Chiles and lemongrass make a transporting marinade for the grilled shrimp. Sliced celery, cucumber, onion, cilantro, and crispy celery leaves get tossed with a sweet, salty, and sour dressing and chopped peanuts. The result is crunchy, tangy, delectable, and filling—and pretty darn healthy, to boot.

2 cloves garlic, peeled and minced

2 bird's eye (Thai) or serrano chiles, stemmed and thinly sliced, divided

2 tablespoons minced lemongrass

4 tablespoons canola oil, divided

¼ teaspoon sea salt

1 pound 26- to 30-count large shrimp, peeled and deveined

3 tablespoons sugar

1 tablespoon fresh lime zest

⅓ cup fresh lime juice

¼ cup Thai fish sauce

3 cups sliced celery stalks (sliced ½ inch thick on a bias)

1 cup celery leaves

½ cup thinly sliced red onion

2 cups sliced seedless cucumber (halved lengthwise, then thinly sliced on a bias)

1 cup fresh cilantro sprigs, plus more for garnish

1 cup chopped roasted peanuts

Place the garlic, 1 sliced chile, the lemongrass, 2 tablespoons of the canola oil, and the salt in a medium bowl. Add the shrimp and stir to coat. Cover and refrigerate for 30 minutes to 1 hour.

Meanwhile, whisk together the sugar, lime zest, remaining sliced chile, the lime juice, fish sauce, and remaining 2 tablespoons canola oil until the sugar dissolves. Set aside.

Remove the shrimp from the refrigerator. Preheat a grill or grill pan over medium-high heat.

Add the shrimp, in batches, if necessary, and cook, flipping once halfway through cooking, until the shrimp are a bright pink-red color but also spotted black from the grill and just cooked through, about 2 minutes per side. Transfer to a plate.

Place the celery stalks, celery leaves, onion, cucumber, and cilantro in a large bowl.

Add the dressing and toss well to combine. Divide the salad among 4 plates and top each with some of the shrimp. Garnish with cilantro springs and the chopped peanuts. Serve immediately.

GLASS NOODLE SALAD WITH PORK, CUCUMBER, AND LEMONGRASS

SERVES 4 | ACTIVE TIME: 40 MINUTES | TOTAL TIME: 50 MINUTES

Noodles, ground pork, and mung bean sprouts fraternize amicably with cold vegetables and fresh herbs before being tossed together in a pungent dressing that's equally spicy, sour, sweet, and salty in this irresistible Thai salad. Quick-cooking mung bean vermicelli is clear and has a fun, chewy texture, making this a brightly flavored, light-colored standout for barbecues and potlucks.

1 (3.52-ounce) package mung bean vermicelli

1 tablespoon fresh lime zest

⅓ cup fresh lime juice

3 tablespoons Thai fish sauce

2 tablespoons finely chopped palm sugar or light brown sugar

4 tablespoons canola oil, divided

½ cup finely chopped shallot

1 bird's eye (Thai) or serrano chile, stemmed and thinly sliced

¼ cup finely chopped fresh lemongrass

2 cloves garlic, peeled and finely chopped

1 pound ground pork

½ teaspoon kosher salt

1 cup mung bean sprouts

½ cup fresh mint leaves, plus more for garnish

½ cup fresh basil leaves, plus more for garnish

2 cups thinly sliced mini cucumbers or seedless cucumbers

1 head Bibb lettuce, stem end trimmed, leaves separated

Lime wedges for serving

Bring a medium saucepan of water to a boil over high heat.

Soak the vermicelli in room-temperature water for 7 minutes, then boil in the water until tender but still chewy, about 3 minutes. Drain, rinse under cold water, then drain again. Using kitchen shears, carefully cut the soft noodles into about 2-inch lengths. Transfer to a large bowl and set aside.

In a small bowl, whisk together the lime zest, lime juice, fish sauce, palm sugar, and 2 tablespoons of the canola oil. Set aside.

Heat the remaining 2 tablespoons canola oil in a large cast-iron or heavy-bottomed skillet over medium-high heat. Add the shallot, chile, and lemongrass and cook until the shallot is soft but not browned, about 2 minutes.

Add the ground pork and salt and break the pork up with a large spoon. Continue to cook, stirring a few times, until browned and crumbly, about 12 minutes. Stir in the garlic and let cook until just warmed through, about another minute, then turn off the heat and transfer to the bowl with the noodles.

Add the mung bean sprouts, cucumber, mint, and basil to the bowl, then pour the dressing over and use tongs to gently toss and coat well in the dressing.

Right before serving, lay the lettuce leaves on a serving platter, top with the salad, and garnish with more fresh mint, basil, and lime wedges. Serve immediately or within a few hours.

SOUPS

RED GAZPACHO

SERVES 4 | ACTIVE TIME: 15 MINUTES | TOTAL TIME: 20 MINUTES

An eating-to-stay-cool cookbook without a gazpacho recipe would be like a tropical cocktail without one of those little umbrellas (it still might be good, but it would seem somehow incomplete). There are seemingly infinite variations of this classic no-cook Spanish hot-weather soup. Some are vegetable-only, but my go-to gazpacho uses a bit of bread (torn into chunks and incorporated into the mix via food processor or blender) to help soak up and evenly disperse the flavors. It also adds a satisfying creaminess, I find. If you'd like a gluten-free version, however, you can simply omit the bread (or use a gluten-free variety).

1 pound ripe tomatoes (about 3 medium), chopped with juices

2 cloves garlic, smashed with the side of a chef's knife and peeled

1 cup torn bread (about 2 ounces) from 1 baguette

2 cups peeled seedless cucumber, plus 1 cup finely chopped for serving

2 cups seeded and chopped red bell pepper (from 2 whole peppers), plus ½ cup finely chopped for serving

1 tablespoon seeded and chopped medium spicy chile, such as Hungarian wax pepper or jalapeño

2 tablespoons chopped fresh flat-leaf parsley, plus more for serving

¼ cup extra virgin olive oil, plus more for drizzling

1 tablespoon sherry vinegar

Sea salt

Freshly ground black pepper

Place the tomatoes and garlic in a food processor or high-powered blender and process until smooth. Add the bread to this mixture, pulse a few times, and let sit until softened, about 5 minutes, then process until smooth.

Add the cucumber, red bell pepper, chile, parsley, and olive oil. Blend on high speed until very smooth and creamy, about 2 minutes.

With the motor running on low, add the vinegar through the hole in the lid. Season with salt and pepper.

To serve, ladle the soup into 4 bowls and garnish with chopped cucumber, red pepper, parsley, and a drizzle of olive oil. Serve immediately or refrigerate in an airtight container for up to 2 days.

WHITE GAZPACHO

SERVES 4 | ACTIVE TIME: 12 MINUTES | TOTAL TIME: 12 MINUTES

Refreshing, cool, and velvety, white gazpacho is a perfect blend of the savory, the sweet, the tangy, and the creamy. Its light color (off-white, in full disclosure) comes from cucumber, fennel, apples, and grapes. Instead of using bread as a thickening agent, white gazpacho derives its creamy texture from almonds—skinless, oily, plump, fragrant Marcona almonds roasted in olive oil and sprinkled with sea salt, to be precise—and is thus both gluten-free and dairy-free (also, delicious).

½ cup Marcona almonds

1 clove garlic, smashed with the side of a chef's knife and peeled

1 teaspoon fresh thyme leaves

1 (12-ounce) seedless cucumber, peeled and chopped (about 2¼ cups)

1 medium fennel bulb (about 8 ounces), trimmed and chopped (about 2 cups)

1 sweet apple, such as Gala, peeled, cored, and chopped

4 ounces white grapes (about ½ cup), plus more, sliced, for serving

1 tablespoon plus 1 teaspoon sherry vinegar

1 cup vegetable broth

⅓ cup extra virgin olive oil, plus more for drizzling

Sea salt

Freshly ground black pepper

Fennel fronds for serving

Place the almonds, garlic, and thyme in a high-powered blender or food processor and blend until very finely chopped, about 1 minute.

Add the cucumber, fennel bulb, apple, grapes, vinegar, vegetable broth, and olive oil and blend on high speed until very smooth and creamy, about 2 minutes. Season with salt and pepper.

To serve, ladle the soup into 4 bowls and garnish with sliced grapes, fennel fronds, and a drizzle of olive oil. Serve immediately, or refrigerate in an airtight container for up to 2 days.

COLD CARROT, CASHEW, AND GINGER SOUP WITH A CRISPY CRUNCHY TOPPING

SERVES 6 TO 8 | ACTIVE TIME: 25 MINUTES | TOTAL TIME: 40 MINUTES

This cool, creamy, spicy, nutty, and completely vegan soup is a tribute to the flavors of India. It features a tantalizing and unexpected zingy topping that will cause your taste buds to rise up and undulate gleefully. In place of cream I've used cashews to thicken and enrich the soup and added nutritional yeast for complexity and depth of flavor. Fried carrot leaves, more cashews, and whole coriander seeds form the basis of the warm, crispy topping whose texture and crunch turbo-inject the soup with liveliness and piquancy. As a courtesy, it's good form to provide advance warning to your guests that there's no going back to everyday, run-of-the-mill carrot-ginger soup after a few spoonfuls of this stuff.

For the soup

2 tablespoons extra virgin olive oil

1 cup chopped yellow onion

Sea salt

Freshly ground black pepper

½ teaspoon cumin seeds

1 tablespoon peeled and grated fresh ginger

2 cloves garlic, smashed with the side of a chef's knife and peeled

1 cup raw unsalted cashews

2 pounds carrots, peeled and cut into ½-inch pieces

2 dried bay leaves

5 cups vegetable broth

2 tablespoons nutritional yeast

For the topping

¼ cup extra virgin olive oil

½ cup raw unsalted cashews, chopped

1 teaspoon coriander seeds

1 cup carrot leaves from carrot stems

Flaky sea salt

To make the soup

Heat the 2 tablespoons olive oil in a large saucepan over medium-high heat. Add the onions, ½ teaspoon sea salt, and ½ teaspoon pepper and cook until just beginning to soften, about 2 minutes.

Stir in the cumin seeds, ginger, garlic, and cashews. Cook until fragrant, about 2 minutes.

Add the carrots, bay leaves, and 1 cup of the vegetable broth. Stir and bring the broth to a simmer. Cover and reduce the heat to medium-low. Cook, stirring once or twice, until the carrots and cashews have softened, about 12 minutes.

Remove the bay leaves and transfer to a high-powered blender in batches with the center cap removed to allow steam to escape, along with the remaining 4 cups vegetable broth and the nutritional yeast. Blend until smooth and transfer to a large bowl. Season with salt and pepper and refrigerate until ready to serve.

To make the topping

Warm the ¼ cup olive oil in a small skillet over medium heat. Add the cashews and cook, stirring occasionally, until lightly toasted, about 2 minutes. Add the coriander seeds and carrot leaves and cook, stirring occasionally, until the leaves begin to crisp, 1 to 2 minutes. Immediately transfer to a bowl and season with flaky salt.

Divide the soup among bowls and garnish each with a few tablespoons of the nut and leaves topping. Serve immediately.

FARMERS MARKET GREENS AND RICE SOUP WITH GINGER AND MISO

SERVES 4 | ACTIVE TIME: 15 MINUTES | TOTAL TIME: 15 MINUTES

This recipe illustrates the age-old culinary principle that when you can't beat the heat, your best bet may be to beat your beet greens instead. Conceived one hot and balmy afternoon after visiting our local farmers market, I invented Farmers Market Greens and Rice Soup as a way to use up a gaggle of greens, including the leafy tops of some beets I'd purchased. Into the blender they went, along with a bowl of leftover rice from the night before, some miso for a hit of umami flavor, spicy fresh ginger, and two vinegars to provide tangy and acidic notes. Eureka—the result of my little experiment was a hearty soup, thanks to the rice, which required no cooking at all, and which provided a perfect balance of sweetness from the lettuce, spinach, and beet greens and spice from the arugula. The already righteous vibes got even groovier when I sprinkled each bowlful with creamy avocado, more shredded fresh greens, and a drizzle of olive oil. Somewhat reminiscent of a green smoothie in the form of a hearty meal, this nutritious soup "leaves" you "chloro-filled" up. "Lettuce produce" some immediately!

3 cups chopped romaine lettuce

3 cups packed spinach leaves

1 cup chopped beet greens (thick stems removed)

1 cup packed arugula leaves

⅓ cup thinly sliced scallions

2 cups vegetable broth

2 cups cooked and cooled sushi rice (you can use leftover rice)

½ cup extra virgin olive oil, plus more for drizzling

2 tablespoons mirin

1 tablespoon sweet white miso paste

1 tablespoon grated fresh ginger

1 tablespoon umeboshi vinegar

1 tablespoon rice vinegar

Sea salt

Freshly ground black pepper

2 cups thinly sliced greens of choice for topping

1 avocado, sliced, for topping

Combine the lettuce, spinach, beet greens, arugula, scallions, and vegetable broth in a high-powered blender. Blend on low speed until the greens are finely chopped, then blend on high speed until smooth.

Add the rice, olive oil, mirin, miso paste, ginger, umeboshi vinegar, and rice vinegar and blend on medium speed until smooth. Season with salt and pepper.

Divide among bowls and top with the thinly sliced greens and avocado and a drizzle of olive oil. Serve immediately or refrigerate in an airtight container for up to 2 days (garnish just before serving).

CAULIFLOWER, PEA, AND LEEK SOUP TOPPED WITH HEIRLOOM TOMATOES, PEA TENDRILS, AND OLIVE OIL

SERVES 4 TO 6 | ACTIVE TIME: 15 MINUTES | TOTAL TIME: 40 MINUTES

Traditional pureed vegetable soups spend a long time on a hot stove. I've got a better method for you (and a splendid recipe, to boot). This soup cooks on low heat through a process called sweating. Essentially you'll be cooking the veggies and aromatics at a low heat to sweat out their flavorful juices; this moisture in turn steams the veggies, so no additional water is required. The beauty of this technique is that all the good flavor is thereby retained, and the result is a velvety and supremely flavorful soup that sidesteps the need for lots of boiling. Serve this soup warm if you wish, but in the depths of the heat I'd advocate eating it either room temperature or, better still, cold. I garnish it with flavorful heirloom tomatoes, pea tendrils, and olive oil. The acidity of the tomatoes adds a perfect contrast to the sweet and creamy soup, green and slightly grassy pea tendrils add texture and a fresh flavor, and a generous drizzle of olive oil provides a spicy and grassy richness. I like to make a batch of this to keep around for a few days, as it makes an easy and hearty meal.

2 tablespoons extra virgin olive oil, plus more for drizzling

1 head cauliflower (about 12 ounces), trimmed and chopped into small pieces

2 leeks, white parts only, halved lengthwise, washed, and thinly sliced crosswise (about 1¾ cups)

2 cloves garlic, smashed with the side of a chef's knife and peeled

1 teaspoon fennel seeds

Sea salt

Freshly ground black pepper

4 cups low-sodium chicken broth or vegetable broth

1½ cups shelled or frozen thawed peas

2 ripe tomatoes, chopped, for garnish

2 cups pea tendrils for garnish

Heat the olive oil in a large pot over low heat. Add the cauliflower, leeks, garlic, fennel seeds, 1 teaspoon salt, and ¼ teaspoon pepper. Stir to coat the vegetables in the oil. Then cover the pot and let the vegetables sweat until the vegetables are cooked through and very tender but not browned, about 20 minutes, stirring a few times during the sweating process.

Stir in 1 cup of the broth and the peas, cover with a lid, and raise the heat to medium. Bring to a simmer and cook until vegetables are completely tender, about 5 minutes.

Transfer the mixture from the pot to a high-powered blender along with the remaining 3 cups broth. You will likely have to do this in batches, due to volume. Transfer the pureed soup to a bowl or serving dish and season to taste with additional salt and pepper.

Serve warm or at room temperature, or refrigerate and serve cold. Top with the chopped tomatoes, pea tendrils, and a healthy drizzle of olive oil. The soup can be kept in an airtight container for up to 4 days and garnished just before serving. Reheat on the stovetop or in a microwave, if desired.

YOGURT SOUP WITH CHICKPEAS, DILL, MINT, GOLDEN RAISINS, CORIANDER, AND SUMAC

SERVES 4 TO 6 | ACTIVE TIME: 20 MINUTES | TOTAL TIME: 20 MINUTES

Looking for an antidote to muggy, humidity-inspired lethargy? This creamy-and-cooling-yet-tangy-and-flavorful Middle Eastern-inspired, no-cook vegetarian soup will wake up your senses and keep you on the qui vive while others begin to wilt, become cantankerous, or—in extreme cases—undergo total psychological decompensation. It starts with a foundation of cooling yogurt, broth, and spices, including nutty, earthy cumin, fragrant coriander, and ground sumac, a tart dried fruit. This recipe raises the flavor and texture stakes by drawing on a quartet of complementary ingredients: chickpeas for heartiness and chew, golden raisins for a touch of sweet, onion for crunch, and fresh dill and mint to add vibrancy and to cut through any richness. Serve by the bowlful as a main course, or dole out smaller portions to kick-start any Mediterranean-themed meal.

3 cups whole milk plain yogurt

3 cups vegetable broth

1½ teaspoons ground coriander

1 teaspoon ground cumin

¼ teaspoon cayenne pepper

½ teaspoon ground sumac, plus more for serving

Sea salt

Freshly ground black pepper

1½ cups drained and rinsed chickpeas (from one 15.5-ounce can)

½ cup chopped red onion

½ cup golden raisins

¼ cup finely chopped fresh mint leaves, plus more for garnish

¼ cup finely chopped fresh dill, plus dill sprigs for garnish

Extra virgin olive oil for drizzling

In a large bowl, combine the yogurt, vegetable broth, coriander, cumin, cayenne, sumac, 1 teaspoon salt, and ½ teaspoon pepper. Whisk to combine.

Add the chickpeas, red onion, raisins, mint, and dill. Stir to combine.

Ladle the soup into 4 bowls and top each with a generous drizzle of olive oil, more mint and dill, a sprinkling of sumac, and more salt and pepper if desired. Serve immediately or within a few hours (garnish just before serving).

CHILLED BORSCHT WITH PUMPERNICKEL CROUTONS, MICROGREENS, CREAM CHEESE FOAM, AND GRATED CURED EGG YOLK

SERVES 4 TO 6 | ACTIVE TIME: 35 MINUTES | TOTAL TIME: 50 MINUTES

I developed my fondness for borscht during a visit to Poland in 1996—somewhat to my surprise. In full disclosure, it was love neither at first sight nor first bite. The only reason I started eating borscht, in fact, was that I was a pescatarian at the time (seafood only, no meat or poultry)—and except for grilled whole fish, which I soon tired of, the vegetarian version of borscht was the only possible menu item for me at many of the meat-heavy restaurants of Krakow and Warsaw. Happily, I quickly realized that genuine borscht is nothing like the watery vermillion stuff I'd tried and hated as a kid. Proper, fresh-made borscht, it turned out, had a rich, earthy flavor that balances sweet, salty, and umami.

My borscht includes several additions—crunchy croutons; fresh, delicate, and slightly spicy microgreens; light and bright-flavored cream cheese foam; and salty cured egg yolks (see page 231)—all of which provide texture, visual interest, and richness to elevate a humble, workaday dish. Serve chilled, by itself, or with a sandwich or toast to round out the meal. To keep it vegetarian, try the Grilled Artichoke Sandwich (page 104). It makes for a light and healthy yet satisfying and filling option when temps are oppressively hot.

Note: Borscht typically takes a long time to cook and boil down, so I've accelerated the process here in various ways, including using a small dice for the vegetables to reduce cooking time.

For the soup

2 tablespoons extra virgin olive oil

1 medium onion, peeled and cut into ½-inch dice (about 1 cup)

3 cloves garlic, smashed with the side of a chef's knife and peeled

¼ cup chopped celery leaves

Sea salt

Freshly ground black pepper

1 pound beets, peeled and cut into ½-inch dice (about 2¼ cups)

1 medium russet potato (about 12 ounces), peeled and cut into ½-inch dice (about 2 cups)

12 ounces carrots, peeled and cut into ½-inch dice (about 2 cups)

2 large celery stalks, cut into ½-inch dice (about 1½ cups)

4 cups vegetable broth

recipe continues on page 96

For the toppings

2 slices pumpernickel bread (about 4 ounces)

2 tablespoons extra virgin olive oil

¼ teaspoon flaky sea salt

4 ounces (½ cup) cream cheese

¼ cup whole milk

1 cup microgreens, such as bull's blood beet greens

2 cured egg yolks (see page 231), grated

To make the soup

Heat the olive oil in a large saucepan over medium-high heat. Add the onion and cook until beginning to soften, about 2 minutes. Add the garlic and celery leaves and cook until just fragrant, about 30 seconds. Season with ½ teaspoon sea salt and ½ teaspoon black pepper.

Stir in the beets, potato, carrots, celery, and 1 cup of the vegetable broth. Bring the broth to a simmer, about 3 minutes, cover with a lid, reduce the heat to medium-low, and cook, stirring once or twice, until the vegetables are very tender, about 15 minutes.

Transfer the mixture, in batches, to a high-powered blender or food processor, along with the remaining vegetable broth. If using a blender, blend on high speed with the center of the lid removed for steam to escape. If using a food processor, process until smooth, about 3 minutes per batch. Transfer the borscht to a large bowl. Cover and refrigerate until ready to serve.

To make the toppings

Place the bread in the toaster and toast until very crisp. Remove from the oven, tear the bread into bite-size pieces, and place in a bowl. Toss with the olive oil and flaky salt, then set aside. The croutons will keep stored in an airtight container at room temperature for up to 5 days.

Place the cream cheese and milk in a high-powered blender or food processor and blend on low speed or process until very frothy and foamy, about 2 minutes. Set aside.

Divide the borscht among bowls and top with the cream cheese foam, croutons, and microgreens. Use a fine grater to grate the cured egg yolk over the top. Serve immediately, or store for up to 5 days in the fridge (garnish just before serving).

CHILLED CORN AND LOBSTER SOUP

SERVES 4 TO 6 | ACTIVE TIME: 45 MINUTES | TOTAL TIME: 3½ HOURS

Between this cookbook's hot weather angle and my status as a Maine resident, neglecting to include at least a couple summery lobster recipes would be risking ostracism, if not exile. Hence this splendid, chilled, lobster-intensive potage, which, I've found, works miracles with out-of-state visitors looking to satisfy their lobster fix. Divvying up the meat from a few whole lobsters among several bowls of hearty, entrée-worthy soup is a great way to stretch out your lobster dollar, incidentally. To heighten the lobster factor even further, I've used the cooking liquid, strained, as the soup's broth, so it's important to remove the rubber bands from your crustaceans' claws prior to cooking. To do so safely, lull them to sleep in the freezer on a small baking sheet for thirty-five to forty-five minutes. This will slow them down so it is easier to remove the bands safely, then transfer the lobsters directly into the boiling water. Along with using the entire lobster, shells and all, here to create the stock, I'm also utilizing all the parts of the corn. There is so much flavor left in the milk and cob of the corn. The milk is the white liquid that, when the cob is pressed, gets extruded. I use the same method for Summer Corn Ice Cream (page 161) to preserve the most possible fresh corn flavor. The irony is, when your guests get their first taste of lobster, corn, herbs, and cream, they'll be pinching themselves to make sure they're not dreaming!

2 dried bay leaves

3 thyme sprigs

Sea salt

Freshly ground black pepper

2 (1½-pound) live lobsters, rubber bands removed (see headnote)

5 ears raw corn, husks and silk removed, corn kernels cut off cobs (about 5 cups kernels), cobs reserved

2 tablespoons extra virgin olive oil

1 shallot, finely chopped

1 clove garlic, peeled and finely chopped

1 cup heavy cream

Chopped fresh herbs, such as tarragon, basil, or chervil, for serving

recipe continues on page 98

In a large pot with lid, combine 5 cups water, the bay leaves, thyme sprigs, 1 teaspoon salt, and ½ teaspoon pepper. Bring to a rolling boil over high heat. Add the lobsters and corn cobs (kernels have been removed and set aside), cover with a lid, reduce the heat to medium, and cook until the lobsters are bright red and cooked through, about 15 minutes. Meanwhile, fill a large bowl of ice and water to create an ice-water bath. Remove the lobsters to the ice water to cool completely.

Use tongs to remove the corncobs from the cooking liquid. Pour the liquid through a fine-mesh strainer into a large pitcher and set aside (there should be about 3½ cups broth).

Meanwhile, use a mallet and kitchen shears to crack the lobster and remove the meat. Any leftover juices can be returned to the pot as extra flavor. Roughly chop the tail meat, then transfer the tail, knuckle, and claw meat to the refrigerator until ready to use (you should have about 2 cups lobster meat).

Warm the olive oil in a large skillet over medium heat. Add the shallot and cook until just soft, about 2 minutes. Add the garlic, corn, and cream and cook, stirring occasionally, until warmed through and the corn has softened, about 8 minutes.

Remove the cooking liquid from the refrigerator. Transfer half of the broth and half of the corn mixture to a high-powered blender and blend until smooth. Transfer to a large serving bowl. Repeat with the remaining cooking liquid and corn. Refrigerate until cold, about 2 hours.

Divide the lobster meat among 4 bowls. Ladle the soup over the top and garnish with fresh herbs. Serve immediately or refrigerate in an airtight container for up to 2 days (garnish just before serving).

TOASTS AND SANDWICHES

CHARRED BROCCOLINI, BURRATA, AND WALNUT PESTO TARTINE ON COUNTRY BREAD

MAKES 4 | ACTIVE TIME: 30 MINUTES | TOTAL TIME: 30 MINUTES

A study in contrasts, this open-faced sandwich balances French and Italian inspirations. Cool, creamy burrata (literally Italian for "buttery") oozes sweetly atop charred Broccolini, crunchy walnut pesto, and pan-toasted crusty country bread. The smoky flavors mellow the Broccolini's slightly bitter, nutty character, but the greens stay bright and snappy. Francophiles can use their favorite runny French cheese and Pistou (page 224).

For the pesto

1 cup raw walnuts

1 clove garlic, peeled

½ cup fresh flat-leaf parsley leaves

½ cup fresh basil leaves

2 tablespoons fresh thyme leaves

¼ cup grated Parmigiano-Reggiano cheese

¼ cup extra virgin olive oil

Sea salt

Freshly ground black pepper

For the tartine

8 ounces Broccolini, rough stem ends trimmed, any thick stems very thinly sliced lengthwise

4 thick slices country loaf

4 teaspoons extra virgin olive oil, plus more for drizzling

8 ounces burrata cheese, divided into 4 pieces

4 peppadew sweet pickled peppers, thinly sliced

Sea salt

Freshly ground black pepper

To make the pesto
Heat a large cast-iron or heavy-bottomed skillet over medium-high heat. Add the walnuts and cook, stirring occasionally, until toasted in parts, 5 to 7 minutes. Transfer to the bowl of a food processor.

Add the garlic to the food processor and process until finely ground, about 30 seconds. Add the parsley, basil, thyme, and Parmigiano-Reggiano cheese and pulse until very finely chopped, about 30 times.

While still processing, slowly drizzle in the ¼ cup olive oil. Transfer to a small bowl and season with salt and pepper. Set aside.

To make the tartine
Wipe the skillet the nuts were in, then heat over high heat. Once the skillet is very hot, just as it begins smoking, add the Broccolini directly to the hot skillet. Cook, using tongs to toss a few times, until the Broccolini is charred in parts and the stems are crisp tender, 4 to 6 minutes. Transfer to a cutting board to rest.

Turn the heat down to medium. Drizzle each bread slice with ½ teaspoon olive oil per side, and working in batches, place on the skillet. Cook, flipping once, until golden and toasted, about 2 minutes per side per batch.

Divide the toasted bread among 4 plates. Spread each with some of the walnut pesto. Top with the Broccolini, burrata, and pickled peppers. Drizzle each tartine more olive oil and sprinkle with salt and pepper. Serve immediately.

GRILLED ARTICHOKE SANDWICHES WITH PICKLES AND JALAPEÑO-ALMOND SPREAD

MAKES 4 | ACTIVE TIME: 40 MINUTES | TOTAL TIME: 40 MINUTES

Artichokes are one of the few vegetables I always keep on hand in the freezer. While I love whole artichokes (especially globes), I find the frozen variety ideal when artichokes appear as merely one of many recipe ingredients. In that context, the idea of boiling them for forty-five minutes to an hour, then breaking them down seems like overkill, especially when it's hot enough to boil an artichoke—I mean, fry an egg—on the sidewalk. In addition, they are considerably lighter than the marinated-in-oil, jarred variety, a plus in the heat. In this sandwich, the hearty, beautifully charred 'chokes play the starring role, buoyed by a strong supporting cast: a rich raw almond and jalapeño spread and crunchy pickles. The roasted flavor of the artichokes, vinegar from the pickles, and richness of the spread provide textures and flavors that collaborate harmoniously. Perfect for a picnic or potluck, this sandwich makes a great light supper as well.

Note: Since this recipe has many components, I recommend making the jalapeño-almond spread and grilled artichokes ahead of time—and, if a scorching day is headed your way, grilling the artichokes early in the morning or at night.

For the spread

1 cup raw almonds

1 jalapeño chile, stem removed and chopped

1 tablespoon nutritional yeast

2 tablespoons extra virgin olive oil

1 tablespoon fresh lemon juice

1 teaspoon garlic powder

1 teaspoon ground cumin

½ teaspoon ground coriander

1 teaspoon sea salt

½ teaspoon freshly ground black pepper

¼ cup water

For the sandwiches

1 (12-ounce) package frozen artichoke hearts, thawed

1 tablespoon extra virgin olive oil

½ teaspoon sea salt

¼ teaspoon freshly ground black pepper

8 slices country loaf, grilled or toasted

1 cup Broccoli and Carrot Ginger Pickles (page 220)

1 cup thinly sliced seedless cucumber

16 large fresh basil leaves

1⅓ cups baby spinach

½ cup radish sprouts

4 radishes, thinly sliced

To make the spread

Process the almonds and jalapeño in a food processor until finely chopped. Add the nutritional yeast, olive oil, lemon juice, garlic powder, cumin, coriander, salt, pepper, and water and process until smooth, about 2 minutes. Set aside.

To make the sandwiches

Drain any water from the thawed artichokes and pat dry with paper towels. Place the artichokes in a medium bowl and gently toss in the olive oil, salt, and pepper.

Heat a grill with a vegetable basket—or a grill pan—over medium-high heat. Oil the grill and grill the artichokes, in batches, if necessary, turning once or twice, until charred in parts, about 6 minutes per batch. Transfer back to the bowl or to a plate.

Place a 13 by 15-inch piece of parchment paper on a surface and place one slice of bread in the middle. Top with ¼ cup of the jalapeño-almond spread, ¼ cup broccoli and carrot pickles, one quarter of the artichokes, ¼ cup sliced cucumber, 4 basil leaves, ⅓ cup spinach, 2 tablespoons radish sprouts, and 1 sliced radish. Top with another slice of bread. The sandwich will be very tall, but wrapping it in parchment paper will hold it all together—and inspire gratitude among your eaters.

Bring the long sides of the parchment paper up tightly to meet in the center. Then fold the short ends over each other as if wrapping a present, and tuck under the sandwich. Repeat this process with the remaining 6 slices of bread to form 3 more artichoke sandwiches, 4 in all. Slice each sandwich in half through the paper, if desired, and serve immediately or within a few hours.

HOME-CURED GRAVLAX, EGG, AND MUSTARD CRÈME FRAÎCHE, WITH GREENS AND HERBS ON PUMPERNICKEL TOAST

MAKES 4 | ACTIVE TIME: 40 MINUTES | TOTAL TIME: 2 DAYS

Curing is a method of preserving and flavoring food that may involve salting, drying, and/or smoking the fare in question—usually meats or seafood—in order to draw water out through osmosis and thus prevent spoilage-causing microorganisms. For the purposes of this book, though, all you really need to know is that the results are tasty and absolutely no cooking is involved. In this recipe you'll be making your own gravlax, i.e., salmon cured in a salt, sugar, herb, and spice mixture, which I've paired with sliced egg, pumpernickel, a simple greens-and-herbs mix, and a creamy, pungent sauce that cuts through the salmon's richness. The work is minimal and the reward is better—and considerably cheaper—than store-bought.

For the gravlax

½ cup sea salt

½ cup sugar

1 tablespoon coarsely ground pink peppercorns

½ cup finely chopped fresh dill

2 tablespoons fresh thyme leaves

12 ounces center-cut salmon fillet, bones removed using tweezers if necessary

For the toasts

4 large eggs

¼ cup crème fraîche

2 tablespoons Dijon mustard

2 cups baby lettuces

½ cup fresh parsley leaves

¼ cup chopped fresh dill

2 tablespoons snipped fresh chives

2 tablespoons extra virgin olive oil

Sea salt

Freshly ground black pepper

4 slices pumpernickel bread, toasted

To make the gravlax

In a medium bowl, stir together the salt, sugar, pepper, dill, and thyme.

Place half of the salt mixture in the bottom of an 8 by 12-inch baking dish lined with a large sheet of wax paper. Place the salmon on top of the salt mixture, skin-side down. Spread the remaining salt mixture evenly over the top of the salmon. Wrap tightly in the wax paper.

Place a few heavy cans on the wrapped salmon to weigh it down. Place in the refrigerator for 24 hours.

Remove the salmon from the refrigerator. Remove the weights, flip the salmon over, replace the weights, and return to the refrigerator to continue curing for another 24 hours.

Unwrap the salmon. Use a spoon or your hands to gently brush off extra salt mixture from the salmon, then rinse and pat dry. Discard any extra brine mixture. Rewrap and return to the refrigerator until ready to use. At this point, the gravlax can be stored in an airtight container in the refrigerator for up to 4 days.

To make the toasts

Prepare a medium bowl of ice water. Place 4 large eggs in a medium saucepan and cover with water by 2 inches. Bring to a boil over high heat. Cover, turn off the heat, and let sit for 7 minutes. Transfer the eggs to the ice water to stop the cooking. Peel the eggs and slice (for tips on peeling eggs, see page 53). Set aside.

In a small bowl, mix together the crème fraîche and mustard. Set aside.

In a medium bowl, gently toss together the lettuce, parsley, dill, and chives with the olive oil. Season with salt and pepper.

Remove the gravlax from the refrigerator and thinly slice across the grain on a bias. Place a few slices on each piece of toast. Top each with a sliced egg, a mound of greens, and a dollop of mustard crème. Serve immediately.

GRILLED SHRIMP WITH HERB BUTTER AND ARUGULA ON CIABATTA TOAST

SERVES 4 | ACTIVE TIME: 25 MINUTES | TOTAL TIME: 55 MINUTES

Elegant and delicious, this toothsome toast is a crowd pleaser for any posh al fresco occasion. If your guests are good eaters, you might consider having more on hand, as this recipe provokes demands for seconds. Who can resist ripe tomatoes marinated in olive oil and white balsamic vinegar, herby compound butter, lemon-and-chile grilled shrimp, and peppery arugula?

1 pound extra-large (16/20 count) shrimp, peeled and deveined (3 to 4 shrimp per toast)

3 tablespoons extra virgin olive oil, divided

¼ teaspoon crushed red chile flakes

1 tablespoon fresh lemon zest

Sea salt

Freshly ground black pepper

6 tablespoons unsalted butter, softened

⅓ cup finely chopped fresh flat-leaf parsley leaves and stems

1 teaspoon chopped fresh thyme leaves

¼ cup thinly sliced fresh basil leaves

1 tablespoon finely chopped fresh oregano leaves

2 medium vine tomatoes (about 12 ounces total), coarsely chopped

1 tablespoon white balsamic vinegar

1 clove garlic, minced

1 (1-pound) ciabatta loaf

1⅓ cups baby arugula

Place the shrimp in a medium bowl. Add 2 tablespoons of the olive oil, the chile flakes, lemon zest, ¼ teaspoon salt, and ½ teaspoon black pepper. Stir to coat the shrimp in the marinade and refrigerate for at least 30 minutes or up to 2 hours.

Meanwhile, in a small bowl, mix together the butter, parsley, thyme, basil, oregano, and ½ teaspoon salt. Set aside.

Place the tomatoes in a medium bowl. Add the vinegar, the remaining 1 tablespoon olive oil, and the garlic. Season with ¼ teaspoon salt and ¼ teaspoon black pepper and toss to combine.

Use a large serrated knife to slice the ciabatta loaf in half crosswise. Then slice each half into 2 slices that are about 3 inches wide by 6 inches long.

Heat a grill or grill pan to medium-high. Place the bread on the grill (in batches if necessary), cut-side down, and cook until grill marks form, 3 to 4 minutes per batch. Place the toasts cut-side up on 4 plates. Let cool slightly, then spread each slice with some of the herb butter and top each slice with ⅓ cup arugula.

Add the shrimp to the grill and cook, flipping once halfway through, until grill marks form and the shrimp are opaque and curled, about 2 minutes per side. Divide the grilled shrimp evenly among the sandwiches, placing them atop the arugula layer.

Evenly sprinkle the chopped tomatoes over the shrimp. Serve immediately.

HEIRLOOM TOMATOES WITH SMOKY TOMATO BUTTER, ROBIOLA, AND MICROGREENS ON SOURDOUGH TOAST

MAKES 4 | ACTIVE TIME: 35 MINUTES | TOTAL TIME: 55 MINUTES

Is there any fresh produce as delicious as a ripe tomato in season? If so, please let me know, because I have yet to come across it. Given these sentiments, it may not surprise you to learn that one of my all-time favorite sandwiches is the simple, ripe tomato sandwich—good bread, fresh tomatoes, butter, and salt—that's it. Some tomato sandwich connoisseurs will make a case for the mayo spread, but for me, softened butter is the perfect foil, helping to counterbalance the acidity of the tomatoes and bring out their natural sweetness.

I've used a smoky sun-dried tomato compound butter here to double the bang for your tomato buck, and just to "gild the lily," robiola cheese—a soft, rich, nutty-flavored, slightly ripe-smelling cheese made with a cow's, goat's, and sheep's milk mixture (good to know in case it comes up at trivia night). Last, I've incorporated microgreens, with a subtle earthiness and tender leaves that nicely complement the other components here. I like combining a few of the many different types of microgreens on the market, but using a single variety is also permissible—opt for whatever is in season.

Not all tomatoes are created equal, of course. I strongly recommend using tomatoes fresh from your garden or the farmers market for this sandwich. And they should be ripe and juicy. If your tomatoes are still a few days away from peak ripeness, make sure to ripen them on the countertop, never in the fridge, which will dry them out and cause them to turn mealy—i.e., unworthy of starring in their very own sandwich. Final hint: This sandwich is an ideal vehicle for those homely or blemished—but otherwise fresh, ripe, and delicious—heirloom tomatoes found at farm stands and green markets, often at a discount. Thinly sliced, covered with robiola and microgreens, and aburst with peak summer flavor, they'll thrill your diners as well as any prize-winning beauty.

recipe continues on page 114

⅓ cup sun-dried tomatoes

4 tablespoons unsalted butter, softened

1 teaspoon smoked paprika

¼ teaspoon sea salt

4 slices sourdough bread, from 1 large sourdough bread loaf

1 pound heirloom tomatoes, thinly sliced into rounds

8 ounces robiola cheese, thinly sliced

½ cup microgreens

Place the sun-dried tomatoes in a bowl and cover with 2 cups hot tap water. Let sit until softened, about 20 minutes. Drain the water and then use your hands to squeeze any additional water out from the tomatoes. Finely chop and transfer to a small bowl.

Add the butter, paprika, and salt. Stir together until a strikingly colored compound butter is formed with swirls of scarlet color from the paprika and tomatoes and yellow-white streaks from the softened butter.

Place the bread in a toaster and toast until golden brown. Let cool to room temperature so the butter doesn't melt.

Spread all 4 slices of bread with the butter. Divide the tomatoes over the top of each, then top with slices of the cheese and a small mound of microgreens. Serve immediately.

PAN-SEARED PORK SANDWICH WITH SPICY PAPAYA SLAW AND SPICY PEPPER JELLY ON SOURDOUGH

MAKES 4 | ACTIVE TIME: 30 MINUTES | TOTAL TIME: 1 HOUR

Find me a more fun double date than hot and spicy with cool and crunchy. Here, the salty-spicy-sweet dry rub perks up lean, fast-cooking, easy-chewing pork tenderloin, paired with Spicy Papaya Slaw (page 61) and Spicy Pepper Jelly (page 228). Perfectly portable for a beach picnic or al fresco potluck, the sandwiches are equally appealing served cold, at room temperature, or warm.

1 tablespoon smoked paprika

2 teaspoons garlic powder

2 teaspoons light brown sugar

1 teaspoon ground cumin

½ teaspoon ancho chile powder

1 teaspoon sea salt

½ teaspoon freshly ground black pepper

1 (1-pound) pork tenderloin, silver skin and excess fat removed

3 tablespoons extra virgin olive oil, divided

8 slices sourdough bread

¼ cup mayonnaise

2 cups Spicy Papaya Slaw (page 61)

¼ cup Spicy Pepper Jelly (page 228)

In a small bowl, combine the smoked paprika, garlic powder, brown sugar, cumin, chile powder, salt, and black pepper.

Pat the pork tenderloin dry with paper towels and then cut it in half crosswise. This helps each end cook more evenly, preventing the narrow end from cooking faster than the thicker end. Rub 1 tablespoon olive oil onto both pieces of tenderloin and sprinkle both all over with the spice rub. Let sit for about 30 minutes on the countertop, until the tenderloin is about room temperature.

Heat a large heavy-bottomed or cast-iron skillet over medium-high heat. Add the remaining 2 tablespoons olive oil and the tenderloin pieces. Sear the tenderloin on all sides, about 4 minutes total, until browned on all sides. Reduce the heat to medium and continue to cook the tenderloin, using tongs to turn a few times, until a digital thermometer inserted into the center of each piece of tenderloin reads 140°F to 145°F—7 to 9 minutes for the narrow piece and 10 to 13 minutes for the wider piece. Remove from the heat. To serve warm, let rest for about 10 minutes. For room temperature pork, let rest about 45 minutes. For cold pork, wrap and transfer to the refrigerator to cool completely, about 1 hour or overnight.

Toast the bread and spread a little mayo on each slice.

Thinly slice the pork tenderloin across the grain and distribute evenly among 4 slices of toast. Top with a mound of spicy papaya slaw. Spread a little hot pepper jelly onto each of the 4 top slices of toast and invert over each sandwich "base" to form 4 sandwiches. Slice each in half and serve.

PAN-SEARED SLICED BEEF, DRESSED DANDELION GREENS, AND HORSERADISH MAYO ON HOMEMADE FLATBREAD

MAKES 4 | ACTIVE TIME: 1 HOUR | TOTAL TIME: 3 HOURS

Flatbread is a great option when you don't even want to think of turning the oven on for hours of baking. After making the dough and letting it rest and rise, it takes mere minutes to cook in a large pan or griddle. Filet is not only delicious and a lean cut, it can be eaten hot, room temperature, or cold since it's easy to slice (and chew). The rich meat and bread are offset by classic steakhouse flavors in the bitter dandelion greens and creamy, spicy horseradish mayo.

For the beef

2 medallions grass-fed filet mignon
(about 1 pound total), at room temperature

2 tablespoons extra virgin olive oil, divided

Sea salt

Freshly ground black pepper

For the flatbread

2¼ teaspoons active dry yeast

¾ cup lukewarm water

2½ cups all-purpose flour

2 teaspoons sugar

1 teaspoon salt

¼ cup extra virgin olive oil, plus more
for brushing the skillet

¼ cup whole milk plain yogurt

For assembly

2 tablespoons jarred prepared horseradish

½ cup mayonnaise

8 ounces dandelion greens, stems removed

2 tablespoons fresh lemon juice

2 tablespoons extra virgin olive oil

Sea salt

Freshly ground black pepper

recipe continues on page 118

To make the beef

Tie the twine tightly around the rim of each of the filet mignons. Pat dry using paper towels. Rub all over with 1 tablespoon of the olive oil and season liberally with salt and pepper all over.

Heat a large cast-iron or heavy-bottomed skillet over high heat. Add the remaining 1 tablespoon olive oil and the beef and sear, turning a few times using tongs, until a brown crust forms on all sides (this beautiful crust will help seal in all the juices), about 8 minutes. Reduce the heat to medium and continue to cook, flipping once halfway through, until a digital thermometer inserted into the center of the meat reads 135°F to 140°F, 4 to 6 minutes per side. Transfer the meat to a cutting board. To serve warm, let rest for about 10 minutes. For room temperature beef, let rest for about 45 minutes. For cold beef, wrap and transfer to the refrigerator to cool completely, about 1 hour or overnight.

To make the flatbread

In a medium bowl, stir the yeast into the lukewarm water. Let it rest until the yeast mixture looks foamy, about 5 minutes.

In a separate medium bowl, stir together the flour, sugar, and salt.

Add the flour mixture, olive oil, and yogurt to the yeast and stir to combine until a shaggy dough forms. Transfer to a large, liberally floured cutting board and knead until a smooth, soft dough forms, about 4 minutes.

Form the dough into a ball and place in a lightly oiled bowl, cover with a cloth, and let rise until doubled in size, about 1 hour. Punch down the dough.

Divide the dough into 4 pieces and use a rolling pin to roll out each piece of dough on the floured cutting board into about 9-inch-diameter rounds.

Heat a large cast-iron skillet over medium-high heat. Lightly brush the skillet with olive oil and add a dough circle to the skillet. Let the dough cook without touching it until bubbles form in the middle of the circle, 1 to 2 minutes. Flip and continue to cook until both sides are cooked through and light brown bubbles form, 3 to 4 minutes total. If the pan gets too hot, reduce the heat to medium. Repeat the process with the remaining pieces of dough.

To assemble

In a small bowl, stir together the horseradish and mayo and set aside. Place the dandelion greens in a medium bowl. Drizzle with the lemon juice and olive oil and gently toss to coat. Season with salt and pepper. Thinly slice the filet mignon across the grain.

Place one flatbread down on a counter and spread with a layer of the horseradish mayo, then add a mound of greens and some slices of the filet mignon. Fold over, wrap in foil, if desired, and serve immediately.

THE SPREAD:
TINNED SEAFOOD

When it's so hot the mere thought of cooking makes you wilt, I've found that putting out a spread is a great solution. In particular, one that features tinned seafood as the headliner can make for a thrown together at the last minute yet stylish and sophisticated meal.

Think beyond just plain canned tuna here: numerous tinned seafood options are delicious and provide the protein you crave without so much as having to touch a button or knob on your stove. In my household you'll find tins of most or all of the following in the pantry at any given time: smoked oysters, kippers, smoked trout, and sardines. If you do want tuna, try one of the Italian fillet varieties that come in glass jars packed in olive oil. For the more ambitious, if you can find Spanish tinned mackerel or clams, you're in for a treat (albeit a rather pricy one). These tins can be found at specialty stores, gourmet markets, and online.

The cold seafood spread is akin to a charcuterie, mezze, antipasti, or cheese platter, in that balancing flavors and textures is paramount. To assemble your spread, get a large cutting board and place an open can or two of tinned seafood on one side. Arrange a few small piles of thinly sliced bread, pita chips, and/or crackers; veggies of some sort; and a few condiment/spread/sauce options. Voila—you've just conjured up a great family-style meal, without breaking a sweat (literally or figuratively).

For your fresh vegetable element, I recommend choosing greens of the peppery or mustardy flavored variety here, which help to cut through and balance out the richness of tinned fish

(typically preserved in oil). Arugula, mustard greens, and radish sprouts are great choices; or make extra dressed dandelion greens and use in this application if making the Pan-Seared Sliced Beef, Dressed Dandelion Greens, and Horseradish Mayo on Homemade Flatbread (page 117). To up the ante further, add a second veg of the crunchy and cooling variety. To name a few, sliced cucumber, shredded carrots, or thinly sliced radish will fit the bill.

Next, add a dollop of something a bit fatty to your bread or crackers—say a ripe, coarsely mashed avocado, crème fraîche, a smear of good butter, or even go a bit further and put out a small ramekin of the Spicy Grilled Eggplant Romesco Dip (page 36).

A bit of heat such as a few drops from a bottle of Cholula or Tabasco, grainy Dijon or spicy mustard, or a bit of Spicy Daikon Pickles (page 223) add a boost.

Speaking of pickles, to add crunch and interest to the spread, pickles or fermented vegetables of some sort are a must, whether homemade or store-bought—check out Garlicky Pickled Red Cabbage (page 219), Broccoli and Carrot Ginger Pickles (page 220), and Quick and Spicy Mediterranean Lemon Pickles (page 217).

Last, I like to liven everything up with a condiment or two. Cucumber Radish Mignonette (page 40) adds a bright vinegary kick, for example; or try a dusting of grated Cured Egg Yolks (page 231) for pure umami. One final word to the wise: those who wash it all down with a crisp dry rosé (see page 200) or hard cider will be glad they did.

RAW CASHEW, SUN-DRIED TOMATO, BEET, AND BASIL ROUNDS

SERVES 4 | ACTIVE TIME: 25 MINUTES | TOTAL TIME: 55 MINUTES

Here's a great no-cook patty with the heft and substance to satisfy the most stubborn burger lovers even when it's too hot to fire up the grill. Serve these flavor-packed rounds on pillow-soft buns with all the fixings. Should your guests eyeball them like uncooked hamburger for their bright-red color, tell them not to fear. The plant-based mixture is delicious, healthy, and versatile—roll smaller for sliders or meatball-sized servings—but unlike most store-bought veggie burgers, not industrially processed, stored frozen in a warehouse, or transported across state lines.

2 cups raw unsalted cashews

1 cup roughly chopped, packed sun-dried tomatoes

1 medium beet (about 6 ounces), peeled and grated (about 1 cup)

1 teaspoon garlic powder

½ cup packed chopped fresh basil leaves, plus more whole leaves for serving

Sea salt

Freshly ground black pepper

1 cup whole milk plain Greek yogurt

½ cup chopped fresh cilantro

¼ cup chopped fresh dill

3 tablespoons chopped fresh mint

1 teaspoon fresh lemon zest

3 tablespoons extra virgin olive oil

4 multigrain buns, toasted if desired

1 cup Garlicky Pickled Red Cabbage (page 219)

1 ripe avocado, pitted, peeled, and sliced

2 cups shredded carrots (from 2 to 3 large carrots) for serving

Place the cashews and sun-dried tomatoes in the bowl of a food processor along with ½ cup hot tap water and let soak until the nuts and tomatoes soften slightly, about 30 minutes.

Process until the nuts and tomatoes are coarsely chopped, then add the beets and garlic powder and process until finely ground, about 2 minutes.

Add the basil, ½ teaspoon salt, and ½ teaspoon pepper. Pulse until combined, about 30 seconds.

Scoop out the mixture and form into 4 even-sized round patties.

In a small bowl, stir together the yogurt, cilantro, dill, mint, lemon zest, and olive oil. Season with salt and pepper.

To serve, spread the yogurt sauce on top of the surface of each bottom bun. Place the "burgers" on top of the sauce. Place basil leaves, pickled cabbage, avocado, and carrots on each patty. Top with the remaining bun halves and a dollop of more sauce, if desired. Serve immediately.

MAIN COURSES

POKE BOWLS WITH PICKLED BOK CHOY, HIJIKI, AND MARINATED SHIITAKE MUSHROOMS OVER SUSHI RICE

SERVES 4 | ACTIVE TIME: 45 MINUTES | TOTAL TIME: 1 HOUR 15 MINUTES

An island specialty, *poke* means simply "to slice" in Hawaiian. Traditionally a simple dish of chopped raw fish with a few seasonings stirred in, more and more elaborate condiments have been added over the years as its popularity has surged into a veritable food trend. I love entertaining with poke—there's no rushing around the kitchen last minute. You can make pretty much everything ahead, except the rice, which tastes best served slightly warm, then your guests simply grab a bowl, add a scoop of rice, and choose their own poke adventure. Since items are mostly raw, pickled, or cooked and cooled, poke parties make a great feast for a hot day. Along with the components below, feel free to try additional toppings, such as cooked edamame, shredded carrots, sliced cucumbers, diced avocado, and toasted sesame seeds.

2 cups sushi rice

For the seasoned hijiki

½ cup dried hijiki seaweed

2 tablespoons mirin

2 tablespoons low-sodium soy sauce

1 tablespoon toasted sesame oil

1 tablespoon toasted sesame seeds

2 teaspoons sugar

For the pickled bok choy

1 pound baby bok choy, stem ends trimmed, sliced crosswise into thin strips (about 4 cups total)

1 teaspoon sea salt

1 teaspoon sugar

For the marinated shiitake mushrooms

8 ounces shiitake mushrooms, stems removed, thinly sliced

¼ cup low-sodium soy sauce

¼ cup dry sake

2 tablespoons sugar

For the poke

2 scallions, thinly sliced

2 teaspoons grated fresh ginger

1 tablespoon low-sodium soy sauce

1 tablespoon toasted sesame oil

¼ teaspoon Korean dried chile flakes or other chile flakes

8 ounces sashimi-grade tuna, salmon, or fish of choice, cut into ½-inch dice

Pickled Ginger (page 222)

recipe continues on page 128

To make the sushi rice

Rinse the rice well in a fine-mesh strainer and steam according to the package directions. Transfer the rice to a bowl and set aside to cool until just slightly warm.

To make the seasoned hijiki

Meanwhile, place the hijiki in a medium bowl, cover with cold water, and let sit until reconstituted, about 30 minutes. Drain well in a large fine-mesh strainer. Run under cold water to clear any debris and drain again. Transfer back to the bowl.

Add the mirin, soy sauce, sesame oil, sesame seeds, and sugar to the hijiki. Stir well to combine. Set aside.

To make the bok choy

Place the bok choy in a large fine-mesh strainer over a large bowl. Add the salt and sugar to the bok choy. Use clean hands to mix well. Let sit until the bok choy softens and liquid drains into the bowl, about 30 minutes.

To make the mushrooms

Combine the mushrooms, soy sauce, sake, and sugar in a medium saucepan and stir gently to coat in the soy sauce mixture. Bring to a simmer over medium heat, about 4 minutes. Stir and continue to cook until the mushrooms are soft and cooked through and the whites take on a light brown pigment, about 5 more minutes. Transfer to a medium bowl and set aside.

To make the poke

In a medium bowl, combine the scallions, ginger, soy sauce, sesame oil, and chile flakes and stir to combine. Add the fish and toss to coat in the mixture.

To serve

Divide the rice among bowls and top each with some of the bok choy, mushrooms, hijiki, poke, and pickled ginger. Serve immediately.

ZARU SOBA (COLD SOBA NOODLES) SERVED WITH MUSHROOM DASHI

SERVES 4 | ACTIVE TIME: 20 MINUTES | TOTAL TIME: 2½ HOURS

This dish of easy-to-slurp noodles and dipping sauce is cold, refreshing, and hugely popular during the hot season in Japan. Soba possess a pleasant chew and slight buckwheat flavor, here complemented by kombu (seaweed), bonito (dried smoked-fish flakes—omit for vegans), and savory dried shiitake mushrooms (all found online or at specialty or Asian markets). The strained broth and slippery noodles are topped with the reconstituted dried shiitakes, thinly sliced cucumbers, radishes, scallions, shredded nori, and sesame seeds.

½ ounce dried kombu seaweed pieces

¼ ounce (about ½ cup) katsuobushi (dried bonito flakes)

1 ounce dried sliced shiitake mushrooms

3 tablespoons sugar

½ cup low-sodium soy sauce

1 pound buckwheat soba noodles

2 cups peeled and julienned seedless cucumber

1 cup thinly sliced radishes

½ cup thinly sliced scallions

¼ cup shredded roasted nori (you could use scissors to shred a sheet of roasted nori)

1 tablespoon toasted sesame seeds

Combine the kombu and 1½ cups water in a small saucepan. Bring just to a boil over high heat, about 3 minutes. Turn off the heat. Add the bonito, cover, and let steep for 10 minutes.

Meanwhile, in a medium saucepan, combine the shiitake mushrooms, sugar, soy sauce, and 2 cups water and bring just to a simmer over medium-high heat, about 8 minutes. Continue to simmer until the

shiitakes are reconstituted and tender, about 4 more minutes. Pour the kombu mixture through a strainer over the mushrooms in the saucepan. Discard the strained kombu and bonito. Transfer the mushrooms and liquid to a medium bowl and refrigerate until cold, about 2 hours or more.

Once the mushroom dipping sauce is cold, strain it through a fine-mesh strainer into a large measuring cup or pitcher; reserve and set aside. Transfer the strained reconstituted and marinated shitakes to a small bowl. Return both the dipping sauce and mushrooms to the refrigerator until ready to serve.

Have a large bowl of ice water ready. Bring a large pot of water to a boil over high heat, about 10 minutes. Cook the soba noodles according to package directions, until just al dente (chewy). Drain. Submerge the noodles in the ice water to stop the cooking process. Drain again.

Divide the noodles among 4 bowls. Top each with the mushrooms, cucumber, radishes, scallions, nori, and sesame seeds.

Pour the dipping sauce into 4 small bowls to serve alongside the bowls of noodles.

To eat, use chopsticks to pick up some of the noodles and vegetables and submerge them in the dipping sauce before eating. Likewise, pour the dipping sauce over each of the noodle bowls. Serve immediately.

COLD KOREAN-STYLE VEGETABLE NOODLES WITH GOCHUJANG AND KIMCHI

SERVES 4 | ACTIVE TIME: 30 MINUTES | TOTAL TIME: 30 MINUTES

My friend Hyeri, who presented me one hot day with a surprising bowl of cold noodles with the perfect balance of heat from chile powder, nuttiness from sesame oil, and tangy funk from kimchi, inspired this recipe. My version uses rice vermicelli noodles, which typically cook by soaking in hot water rather than boiling (or else require just a few minutes of boiling).

6 ounces rice vermicelli noodles

6 tablespoons toasted sesame oil, divided

1 cup peeled and grated Anjou pear
(from 1 or 2 firm but ripe pears)

1 tablespoon peeled and grated fresh ginger

1 clove garlic, peeled and finely chopped

¼ cup gochujang

2 tablespoons sweet white miso

3 tablespoons soy sauce

1 tablespoon mirin

2 teaspoons sugar

1½ teaspoons unseasoned rice vinegar

5 tablespoons canola oil, divided

7 ounces shiitake mushrooms, stems removed
and thinly sliced

3 scallions, thinly sliced, white, light green,
and dark green parts divided

2 large carrots, peeled and grated using a
serrated vegetable peeler

1 bunch lacinato kale (about 10 ounces), stems
removed, leaves thinly sliced

1 cup thinly sliced seedless cucumber

1 cup kimchi and/or Spicy Daikon Pickles
(page 223)

1 teaspoon toasted sesame seeds

Cook the noodles according to the package directions. Run under cold water to stop the cooking process, then drain well and use your hands to squeeze out any excess water. Transfer to a large bowl and toss the noodles with 2 tablespoons of the sesame oil to prevent sticking. Set aside.

Meanwhile, place the pear, ginger, garlic, gochujang, miso, soy sauce, mirin, sugar, vinegar, remaining 3 tablespoons sesame oil, and 2 tablespoons of the canola oil in a medium bowl and stir to combine. Set aside.

Heat 1 tablespoon of the remaining canola oil and 1 teaspoon of the remaining sesame oil in a large skillet over medium-high heat. Add the shiitakes and cook until the whites of the mushrooms are golden, about 4 minutes.

Add 1 tablespoon of the remaining canola oil, 1 teaspoon of the remaining sesame oil, and the scallion whites and light green parts to the skillet and cook, stirring occasionally, until tender, about 2 minutes. Add the carrots and cook, stirring occasionally, until crisp tender, about 3 minutes. Pour the carrot mixture into the reserved noodles in the bowl.

Add the remaining 1 tablespoon canola oil and 1 teaspoon sesame oil to the skillet. Add the kale and cook, stirring occasionally, until just wilted, about 3 minutes. Add to the bowl with the vegetables and noodles along with the cucumber. Add the sauce to taste and toss to combine well.

Divide the noodles among 4 bowls. Top each with some of the kimchi, scallion greens, and toasted sesame seeds. Serve immediately.

COLD POACHED ARCTIC CHAR WITH HERB, WALNUT, AND MIXED CITRUS QUINOA SALAD

SERVES 4 | ACTIVE TIME: 50 MINUTES | TOTAL TIME: 1 HOUR 20 MINUTES

The dish features arctic char, a moist and flaky fish with an orange-hued flesh that can range from pale to vibrant. Though closely related to salmon, I find that arctic char tends to be a little less fatty, so if you're looking for seafood on the lighter side, give it a try. If you have trouble locating arctic char, other rich-fleshed fish that would work well in this recipe include salmon, halibut, cod, trout, or striped bass. The fish poaches in a mixture of herbs, wine, aromatics, and spices, then chills in the poaching liquid, giving the flavors ample opportunity to intermingle and absorb. Finally, the chilled fish is served atop a bed of earthy quinoa, toasted walnuts, fresh herbs, and citrus segments of your choosing. The resulting dish is healthy, refreshing, and satisfying.

For the fish

1½-pound piece skinless center-cut arctic char, pin bones removed, cut into 4 pieces

Sea salt

1 cup dry white wine

2 cups seafood stock

3 dried bay leaves

1 teaspoon whole black peppercorns

1 shallot, peeled and thinly sliced

6 cloves garlic, smashed with the side of a chef's knife and peeled

6 sprigs fresh flat-leaf parsley

3 sprigs fresh thyme

For the quinoa salad

1 cup quinoa

Sea salt

5 tablespoons extra virgin olive oil, divided

1 cup raw walnuts

1 cup mixed citrus fruit segments, such as grapefruit, orange, and tangerine

1 cup fresh flat-leaf parsley leaves, plus more for garnish

½ cup coarsely chopped fresh dill, plus more for garnish

½ cup fresh mint leaves, plus more for garnish

¼ cup snipped fresh chives

2 tablespoons fresh lemon juice

Freshly ground black pepper

Lemon wedges, for serving

To make the fish

Sprinkle the arctic char all over with ¾ teaspoon salt and set aside.

Combine the wine, seafood stock, bay leaves, peppercorns, shallot, garlic, parsley, thyme, and ½ teaspoon salt in a large high-sided skillet. Cover with a lid and bring to a rolling boil over medium-high heat, about 12 minutes.

Remove the lid and add the fish to the skillet. Reduce the heat to medium, cover, and continue to simmer until the fish is just cooked through, 5 to 7 minutes.

With the lid off, let the fish cool to room temperature, about 30 minutes. Transfer the skillet to the refrigerator, uncovered, and let cool completely, about 1 hour.

To make the quinoa

Meanwhile, combine the quinoa, 2 cups water, and 1 teaspoon salt in a medium saucepan. Bring to a boil over high heat, cover, reduce the heat to low, and cook until the water is absorbed and the quinoa is cooked through, about 15 minutes.

Transfer the quinoa to a large fine-mesh strainer. Run under cold water to stop the cooking process. Drain well and transfer to a medium bowl.

Heat 2 tablespoons of the olive oil in a medium skillet over medium-high heat. Add the walnuts and cook, stirring occasionally, until toasted, 3 to 4 minutes.

Transfer the nuts to the bowl with the quinoa. Add the citrus, parsley, dill, mint, chives, the remaining 3 tablespoons olive oil, and the lemon juice. Gently stir to combine and season with salt and pepper.

To serve

Divide the quinoa salad among 4 plates or bowls and top each with some of the arctic char. Discard any poaching liquid. Garnish each plate with more fresh herbs and a couple lemon wedges. Serve immediately.

COCONUT MILK, TURMERIC, GINGER, AND BLACK PEPPER–POACHED COD WITH ISRAELI COUSCOUS

SERVES 4 | ACTIVE TIME: 40 MINUTES | TOTAL TIME: 40 MINUTES

Poaching—the legal kind—is a moist-heat cooking process by which food is gently simmered in anything from plain water to broth, milk, bouillon, or other flavorful liquids. It's an ideal technique for keeping intact delicate foods like eggs and fish that might otherwise break up during the cooking process. I love this recipe's variety of textures and flavors: delicate cod, chewy pearls of couscous, spicy and creamy coconut milk broth, with herbs and lime adding a fresh, vibrant finish. Fresh turmeric root, ginger root, spicy chiles, and black peppercorns liven up coconut milk and seafood stock as the poaching medium. This is an example of a "heating to cool"–type dish, in which spice and heat induce the eater to sweat out the heat (see page 60). If you haven't tried fresh turmeric, by the way, you are in for a treat. Above and beyond its lovely, warm yellow color, the fresh stuff boasts a pleasant, slightly fruity and floral flavor, and numerous health benefits, including potent anti-inflammatory and antioxidant qualities.

For the fish

4 (6-ounce) pieces center-cut cod fillet, pin bones removed

Sea salt

3⅓ cups coconut milk (two 13.5-ounce cans)

1½-ounce piece fresh unpeeled turmeric, thinly sliced (or 1 tablespoon ground turmeric)

1½-ounce piece fresh unpeeled ginger, thinly sliced

4 cloves garlic, smashed with the side of a chef's knife and peeled

1 shallot, peeled and thinly sliced

2 serrano chiles, stems removed, sliced in half lengthwise

1 tablespoon light brown sugar

1 teaspoon whole coriander seeds

½ teaspoon whole black peppercorns

For the couscous

1 tablespoon virgin (unrefined) coconut oil

1 cup Israeli couscous

1½ cups seafood stock

2 scallions, thinly sliced, for serving

1 cup fresh cilantro sprigs for serving

8 lime wedges for serving

recipe continues on page 136

To make the fish

Sprinkle the cod lightly all over with ¾ teaspoon salt and set aside.

Combine the coconut milk, turmeric, ginger, garlic, shallot, serrano chiles, brown sugar, coriander, black peppercorns, and 1 teaspoon salt in a large high-sided skillet. Stir to combine, cover with the lid, and bring to a simmer over medium heat, 12 to 15 minutes.

Remove the lid, stir, and add the cod to the skillet. Cover with the lid again and continue to cook until the fish is just cooked through, 8 to 10 minutes. Remove the lid and set aside.

To make the couscous

While the fish cooks, melt the coconut oil in a medium saucepan over medium-high heat.

Add the couscous and cook, stirring occasionally, until the couscous is toasted in parts, about 2 minutes.

Add the stock and bring to a boil. Cover, reduce to a simmer, and cook, stirring a few times during cooking, until tender, about 10 minutes.

To serve

Divide the couscous among 4 large bowls. Top each with a piece of fish and spoon a good amount of coconut cooking broth over the top. Garnish with scallions, cilantro, and lime wedges and serve immediately.

PASTA WITH CRAB, HERBS, AND CHILES

SERVES 4 | ACTIVE TIME: 30 MINUTES | TOTAL TIME: 30 MINUTES

If you are a crab enthusiast, this spicy, lemony, herby, crabby pasta will have your mouth watering and your body sweating out the heat (to avoid dehydration, best keep a water bottle handy—or, better yet, an ice-cold, super-dry white or rosé from the Mediterranean region). It can be served either hot or at room temperature. I've gone with thin spaghetti here to reduce cooking time. Speaking of which, a few general notes on boiling water. First, covering with a lid significantly speeds up the time it takes to reach a boil. Second—hopefully this is obvious—always use high heat. Third, the oft-repeated truism that cold water boils faster is a myth that should be taken with a (crabby) pinch of sea salt. And fourth, this dish is so dang delicious that anyone who complains can go eat outside.

Sea salt

1 pound thin spaghetti

6 tablespoons extra virgin olive oil, divided

2 cups freshly torn breadcrumbs from 1 baguette (about 3 ounces; crumbs should be large—you want jagged nooks and crannies)

2 cloves garlic, peeled and thinly sliced

1 Fresno, jalapeño, or serrano chile, stem removed and thinly sliced

1 pound fresh jumbo lump crabmeat, with any small bits of shell picked out and removed

1 tablespoon fresh lemon zest

½ cup finely chopped fresh flat-leaf parsley leaves

2 tablespoons fresh lemon juice

Freshly ground black pepper

Bring 4 to 5 quarts water to a boil over high heat in a large covered pot. Add a generous amount of salt to the cooking water (about ¼ cup). Add the pasta, stir, and cook just until al dente, about 7 minutes (or according to package directions). Reserve 1 cup of the pasta water and drain the pasta.

Meanwhile, heat 2 tablespoons of the olive oil in a large, high-sided skillet over medium-high heat. Add the breadcrumbs and cook until golden and lightly toasted, about 4 minutes. Season lightly with salt and transfer to a small bowl.

Using the same large, high-sided skillet the breadcrumbs were cooked in, heat the remaining 4 tablespoons olive oil with the garlic and chile over medium heat until the garlic begins to soften, 1 to 2 minutes. Add the crabmeat and lemon zest and cook, gently stirring, until heated through, 2 to 3 minutes.

With the heat off, add the pasta to the pan along with the reserved pasta water, parsley, and lemon juice. Use tongs to gently toss and combine the ingredients. Season with salt and pepper.

Divide the pasta among 4 bowls and top each with some of the breadcrumbs. Serve immediately.

GRILLED CHICKEN AND SWEET POTATO STREET TACOS WITH RADISH, PICKLED RED CABBAGE, AND BLACK BEANS

SERVES 4 | ACTIVE TIME: 45 MINUTES | TOTAL TIME: 45 MINUTES

Street tacos are smaller than your average taco and typically served open-faced on soft corn tortillas with the fillings exposed, two to three on a plate. This format facilitates quick cooling and makes for a portable, on-the-go meal, since each taco can be folded and eaten in a few hearty bites. Traditionally sold from carts or food trucks, street tacos often arrive "two-ply," i.e., with a secondary, extra soft taco (usually corn) stacked under the first to help prevent messy accidents resulting from tortilla collapse or implosion. My own preference is for a single tortilla (in full disclosure, because it means I can eat more tacos before I get full), but the solo vs. dual tortilla decision is a personal one that each of us must make. The sweet and savory tacos in this recipe are filled with smoky slices of dry-rubbed, dark meat chicken, thinly sliced sweet potatoes, cold and creamy black beans, fresh herbs, Garlicky Pickled Red Cabbage (see page 219), crunchy sliced radishes, and salty, crumbly cotija cheese. Cotija cheese can be found in Mexican markets, gourmet markets, or cheese shops. Add a fresh squeeze of lime and let the celebración begin!

4 boneless skinless chicken thighs
(1 to 1¼ pounds total)

1 medium sweet potato (about 10 ounces), peeled, halved lengthwise, and cut into ¼-inch-thick slices

1 tablespoon light brown sugar

2 teaspoons smoked paprika

1 teaspoon chipotle chile powder

1 teaspoon garlic powder

1½ teaspoons ground cumin, divided

½ teaspoon ground coriander

Sea salt

Freshly ground black pepper

4 tablespoons extra virgin olive oil, divided, plus more for the grill

1 (15.5-ounce) can black beans, drained and rinsed

½ cup chopped fresh cilantro, plus fresh cilantro sprigs for serving

2 teaspoons fresh lime zest

8 to 16 small corn tortillas

1 cup Garlicky Pickled Red Cabbage (page 219)

8 radishes, thinly sliced

½ cup crumbled cotija cheese for serving

Lime wedges for serving (optional)

recipe continues on page 142

Place the chicken thighs in a large baking dish and the sweet potatoes in another. Set aside.

In a small bowl, stir together the brown sugar, paprika, chile powder, garlic powder, 1 teaspoon of the cumin, the coriander, 2 teaspoons salt, and 1 teaspoon pepper.

Sprinkle half of the spice mixture onto the chicken and the other half onto the sweet potatoes. Drizzle each with 2 tablespoons olive oil and toss each to coat in the spice mixture. Let sit for 15 minutes at room temperature.

Meanwhile, in a medium bowl, combine the black beans with the ½ cup cilantro, the lime zest, remaining ½ teaspoon cumin, and ¼ teaspoon salt. Stir to combine.

Preheat a grill or grill pan to medium-high and oil the grates of the grill. Place the sweet potatoes on the grill (in batches, if necessary) and cook, flipping once halfway through, until tender and grill marks have formed on both sides, about 4 minutes per side.

Place the chicken on the grill and cook, flipping once halfway through, until the chicken has an internal temperature of 165ºF and grill marks have formed, about 7 minutes per side. Transfer to a cutting board and let rest for 5 to 10 minutes, then slice across the grain into strips.

Warm up the tortillas by putting them directly on the gas burner of a stove or on the grill pan with the heat on medium. Use tongs to turn and flip them until soft and pliable and slightly charred in parts, about 1 minute per tortilla.

Divide the tortillas among 4 plates. Top each with chicken, sweet potatoes, beans, pickled cabbage, radishes, and cotija cheese. Garnish with cilantro sprigs and a squeeze of lime, if desired.

QUICKER ROASTED LEMON AND HERB CHICKEN WITH DRIPPING CROUTONS AND WILTED GREENS

SERVES 4 | ACTIVE TIME: 50 MINUTES | TOTAL TIME: 1½ HOURS

If you're like me, the glorious flavor of roast chicken is one you may find yourself craving whether it's New Year's, the Fourth of July, or anytime in between. When this happens and heat lines are rising from the sidewalk outside, the obvious solution is to head for an air-conditioned market and make a beeline for the precooked rotisseries. I fully support this approach—rotisserie chicken makes a versatile base for countless recipes (see page 147). But—real chicken talk—the truth is that, taste-wise, nothing quite beats homemade roast chicken from your own oven. The recipe that follows will deliver a fabulous result, while significantly reducing oven time. To help accomplish this, I've forgone the whole bird in favor of chicken thighs, a strategic choice, since the meat is moist and won't dry out.

What's more, this recipe delivers a bonus that your business-as-usual rotisserie doesn't, namely homemade dripping croutons. If you're not familiar with dripping croutons, they are essentially baguette discs that are flavored with the bird's flavorful juices, or "drippings," (hence the name) and added to the pan mid-roast, to bake along with the bird. The result is a mouthwatering side with a texture that's simultaneously crunchy and soft. To round things out here, the chicken and croutons are served with wilted spicy and mustardy-flavored greens of choice, sautéed with garlic and lemon. As they cook, the flavors from all three components will mingle, bond, and get on like a house on fire . . . even as yours stays relatively cool.

¾ baguette (about 6 ounces), sliced crosswise 1 inch thick

¼ cup finely chopped fresh flat-leaf parsley leaves and stems

1 tablespoon fresh lemon zest

1 tablespoon finely chopped fresh rosemary leaves

¼ teaspoon crushed red chile flakes

8 tablespoons extra virgin olive oil, divided

Sea salt

Freshly ground black pepper

8 bone-in, skin-on chicken thighs (about 3 pounds total)

2 cloves garlic, peeled and thinly sliced

1 pound greens of choice, such as kale, mustard greens, or broccoli rabe, rough stems trimmed, leaves coarsely torn (about 5 cups packed greens)

1 tablespoon fresh lemon juice

recipe continues on page 145

Place the baguette slices in a large bowl and set aside.

Combine the parsley, lemon zest, rosemary, red chile flakes, 4 tablespoons of the olive oil, 1 teaspoon salt, and ½ teaspoon black pepper in a small bowl and stir until combined.

Pat the chicken dry using paper towels. Use your fingers to gently separate and loosen the skin of the thighs and slide the herb mixture under the skin. Rub some of the paste onto the outside as well and place on a cutting board. Season the outside of all the chicken thighs liberally with more salt and pepper. Let sit at room temperature for about 20 minutes.

Meanwhile, center a rack in the oven, place a baking sheet on the rack, and preheat the oven to 425°F.

Heat a large cast-iron or heavy-bottomed skillet over medium-high heat. When the pan is very hot, add 2 tablespoons of the remaining olive oil to the pan, place half of the chicken thighs in the pan skin-side down, and cook until browned, 3 to 4 minutes. Flip over and continue to brown for 3 to 4 more minutes, then transfer to a plate. Repeat with the second batch.

Use tongs to carefully transfer the chicken thighs skin-side up to the baking sheet in the oven, spacing them out to cook evenly. Pour any juices and oil accumulated in the skillet over the bread in the bowl and toss to combine. Set aside. Reserve the skillet (this will get used for cooking the greens).

Roast the chicken for about 10 minutes, then carefully add the croutons to the baking sheet with the chicken, along with any juices in the bowl. Continue to cook until a digital thermometer inserted into the thickest part of the chicken thighs not touching the bone reads 165°F, 5 to 10 minutes more. Remove from the oven and let rest.

Meanwhile, add the remaining 2 tablespoons olive oil and the garlic to the reserved skillet and cook, stirring and scraping the browned bits in the pan with a large spoon, until the garlic is fragrant and begins to soften, about 2 minutes. Add the greens, in batches if necessary, and use tongs to toss until slightly wilted, 2 to 6 minutes per batch, depending on the type of greens used.

Add the lemon juice, season with salt and pepper, and toss until combined.

Divide the chicken among 4 plates along with the croutons and wilted greens. Serve immediately.

FUN WITH A
ROTISSERIE CHICKEN

If you are craving roast chicken but it's simply too hot to face the thought of turning on the oven (even for Quicker Lemon and Herb Roasted Chicken with Dripping Croutons and Wilted Greens, page 143), I understand and sympathize. In the midst of summer's dog days, the idea of an indoor roasting session can be off-putting, if not a total nonstarter. Grilling is great, but city dwellers often lack easy access to an outdoor cooking situation and, of course, grilled chicken has its own, separate flavor profile. When presented with such a predicament, the supermarket rotisserie chicken can be a godsend. Let's face facts, bought rotisserie chickens are inexpensive, tasty, and super-convenient, especially when you want to avoid touching the stove. My purpose here is to encourage you to expand your rotisserie consciousness a bit. You can eat store-bought roast chickens as is, certainly, but as the concepts below illustrate, they also can be repurposed for a wide range of satisfying, no-sweat summer meals.

THE GREEN SMASH

Mash an avocado, stir in lime juice, cilantro, red grapes, and green onion, add shredded chicken, and season with salt and pepper for a mayo-free chicken salad.

VIETNAMESE STREET FOOD

Mix shredded chicken with shredded carrots, shredded purple cabbage, mint, lime juice, soy sauce, and toasted sesame oil and serve in lettuce leaves for a quick Vietnamese-style lettuce wrap.

MAKE IT CHICKEN SOUP

Top cold soup (see pages 83 to 99) with chilled shredded chicken for added protein.

QUICKER SHAWARMA

Thinly slice rotisserie chicken breast and lightly sprinkle all over with ground cumin and coriander, salt, and pepper. Wrap up in a warm pita with harissa sauce and/or Toasted Garlic, Ginger, and Chile Oil (page 227), a couple spoonfuls of Greek yogurt, chopped lettuce, and tomato for a quick shawarma-style sandwich.

THE PERFECT PICNIC

Serve cold chicken legs as a classic addition to a picnic basket. Bring sauce options for dipping, such as Spicy Pepper Jelly (page 228) or Herby Pistou (page 224).

MAKE IT CHICKEN PASTA

Toss shredded chicken and leftover pasta in olive oil, lemon juice, crushed red chile flakes, fresh herbs, salt, and pepper for a quick and tasty pasta salad.

GRILLED MARINATED SKIRT STEAK AND BARLEY SALAD WITH DRIED CHERRIES, FRESH HERBS, AND LEMON PICKLE

SERVES 4 | ACTIVE TIME: 40 MINUTES | TOTAL TIME: 1 HOUR 40 MINUTES

When it's hot out and you find yourself with a yen for red meat, I urge you to consider the humble skirt steak, for three primary reasons: First, it's very thin and thus cooks quickly, whether on the grill or in a skillet. Second, it's a lean cut, and thus will keep you cooler than a fattier alternative like rib eye. Third, the skirt steak's coarse surface makes it an effective sponge for sopping up herbs, spices, and marinades—a distinct plus for flavor-intense recipes like this whole-grain salad.

As for the whole grain, I've chosen barley, with a densely textured chew that I find delightful. Barley takes up to an hour to cook, so I'm using the pre-steamed, quick-cook variety here to speed things along. Finally, for added allure, I've included a bevy of complementary flavors to enhance barley's neutral profile, with sweet-tart dried cherries, salty pickled lemon (page 217), and fresh herbs most prominent among them.

2 tablespoons Worcestershire sauce

1 tablespoon soy sauce

4 cloves garlic, smashed with the side of a chef's knife and peeled

1 tablespoon chopped fresh thyme leaves

2 teaspoons chopped fresh rosemary leaves

2 teaspoons light brown sugar

1¼ pounds skirt steak, excess fat trimmed, cut in half crosswise

Sea salt

Freshly ground black pepper

2 cups quick-cooking barley

¼ cup extra virgin olive oil, plus more for the grill

½ cup dried unsweetened cherries

2 tablespoons chopped lemon peel from Quick and Spicy Mediterranean Lemon Pickles (page 217)

1 cup fresh flat-leaf parsley leaves

1 cup torn fresh basil leaves

recipe continues on page 150

Place the Worcestershire sauce, soy sauce, garlic, thyme, rosemary, and brown sugar in a large resealable bag. Add the skirt steak halves, seal the bag, and massage to coat the steak evenly in the marinade. Marinate in the refrigerator for at least 1 hour or or overnight.

Remove the steak from the refrigerator and sealed bag. Discard the marinade and pat the steak dry with paper towels. Season the steak all over with salt and pepper. Let rest at room temperature for about 30 minutes before grilling.

Meanwhile, in a large saucepan, combine the barley with 5½ cups water and 1 tablespoon salt and bring to a boil over high heat, 5 to 6 minutes. Reduce the heat to low, cover, and cook until just tender, about 10 minutes. Drain the barley in a fine-mesh strainer and run under cold water to stop the cooking process. Drain again and transfer to a medium bowl. This step can be done up to 1 day ahead of time, if desired.

Add the olive oil, cherries, lemon pickle, parsley, and basil. Season with salt and pepper. Set aside.

Preheat a grill or grill pan to high heat and oil the grill grates. Place the two pieces of meat on the grill and let cook without moving until grill marks form and the meat looks dark brown and caramelized, 2 to 3 minutes. Flip and continue to cook until the meat has an internal temperature of 145ºF, 2 to 3 minutes more.

Take off the heat and let rest for about 10 minutes before slicing across the grain.

To serve, divide the barley salad among 4 bowls and top each with some of the sliced skirt steak, distributing the meat evenly among the bowls. Serve immediately.

DESSERTS

CHOCOLATE PANNA COTTA WITH SALTY PRALINE PEANUT CRUMBLE

MAKES 8 INDIVIDUAL-SIZE PANNA COTTAS | ACTIVE TIME: 25 MINUTES | TOTAL TIME: 5 HOURS

Panna cotta, a creamy and cold dessert, literally translates from the Italian as "cooked cream." Though comparable to custard in texture, panna cotta is thickened using gelatin rather than egg. This results in a fun, flan-like jiggle, and once removed from its ramekin mold, panna cotta looks elegant on the plate. My panna cotta incorporates semisweet and milk chocolate, a departure from the usual bittersweet, and is topped with crunchy, salty praline peanut crumble tossed in quick homemade caramel—an ideal accompaniment to the creamy, rich chocolate. Since chocolate is the hero of this dessert, make sure you buy the best quality.

For the panna cotta

Cooking spray or canola oil for the ramekins

2¾ cups heavy cream

1 (.25-ounce) packet gelatin (2¼ teaspoons)

¼ cup sugar

⅛ teaspoon sea salt

3 ounces milk chocolate, finely chopped (about ½ cup)

2 ounces semisweet chocolate, finely chopped (about ⅓ cup)

For the salty praline peanut crumble

Cooking spray

½ cup sugar

2 tablespoons water

½ cup roasted salted peanuts

To make the panna cotta

Spray or brush 8 (6-ounce) ramekins with canola oil. Place them on a small baking sheet and set aside.

Pour ½ cup of the cream into a small bowl, sprinkle in the gelatin, and gently stir to combine. Let rest for about 8 minutes, until the gelatin has softened and bloomed.

Combine the remaining 2¼ cups cream, the sugar, and salt in a small saucepan and bring just to a boil over high heat, stirring occasionally. Turn off the heat and pour in the gelatin mixture and chocolate. Let sit for about 5 minutes for the chocolate to melt, then whisk until combined and completely smooth. Strain through a fine-mesh strainer into a large measuring cup.

Divide the panna cotta among the ramekins. Let cool slightly, about 20 minutes, then transfer to the refrigerator to cool and set completely, about 4 hours or overnight. At this stage, you can wrap the panna cottas in plastic wrap and refrigerate for up to 3 days.

recipe continues on page 156

To make the crumble

Line a standard-sized baking sheet with parchment paper or a Silpat baking mat. If using parchment, spray it all over with cooking spray. Set aside.

In a medium saucepan, stir together the sugar and water. Use a pastry brush dipped in water to brush around the insides of the pan to remove any sugar crystals that form.

Cook over medium-high heat without stirring until the caramel is a medium-amber color, 6 to 8 minutes. Immediately and carefully add the nuts to the saucepan. Stir to coat the nuts, then spread them out on the baking sheet. Let cool until hardened, about 30 minutes. Transfer to a food processor and pulse until finely chopped. The crumble can be kept in an airtight container at room temperature for up to 1 week.

To serve

Have a medium bowl of hot water ready. Dip each ramekin into the hot water for 10 to 20 seconds, then use an offset spatula around the inner rim of the panna cotta to loosen. Place the serving plate on top of the ramekin with the panna cotta in it and flip over to release onto a plate. Sprinkle each panna cotta with some of the praline. Serve immediately.

HOW (AND WHY) TO MAKE YOUR OWN RICOTTA

MAKES 2 CUPS

ACTIVE TIME: 20 MINUTES

TOTAL TIME: 1 HOUR

Do-it-yourself ricotta cheese is one of those high-return-on-investment culinary items: for the minimal amount of effort it requires, there's a dramatic payoff—a quantum leap forward in quality, texture, and taste. Homemade ricotta—even amateur homemade ricotta—is simply fresher, creamier, and much superior to the standard purchase. Once you've tried the real deal, in fact, it's hard to go back to the garden-variety plastic-tub kind. And that's OK, because making your own ricotta is a cinch. True, you may be able to find a high-end, small-batch, store-purchased ricotta, but you'll be paying through the nose—and chances are it still won't be nearly as good. Skimming the recipe below should give you a feel for just how simple it is—and, I hope, inspire you to give it a whirl. For many readers, I suspect the sole unfamiliar element of this recipe may be the cheesecloth used to strain off the whey (milky liquid) after the curds form. You can skip this step if you are a disciple of Little Miss Muffet and prefer to eat whey with your curds—but otherwise, you'll need cheesecloth, which can be purchased at practically any supermarket.

I urge you to try this homemade version when ricotta is called for in recipes such as the Pistachio, Strawberry, Lemon, and Ricotta Gelato (page 158) or the Malted Chocolate Icebox Cake (page 173). If there's any left over—or if you simply prefer not to be bogged down by external distractions, try spreading a big glob on a thick piece of toast with some good olive oil, flaky salt, and pepper: it's a killer five-minute snack. To make a meal of it, you can add a side salad such as the Matchstick Apple, Jicama, and Fennel Slaw with Honey Lemon Vinaigrette (page 59). Yet another idea: if you can't locate burrata when making the Charred Broccolini, Burrata, and Walnut Pesto Tartine, substitute homemade ricotta instead. You say burrata? I say ricotta.

Note: For the cream in this recipe I recommend seeking out heavy cream with no additives, as additives can adversely affect the ricotta's texture and flavor.

4 cups whole milk

1½ cups heavy cream

5 tablespoons distilled white vinegar

Sea salt

Have ready a large bowl topped with a large fine-mesh strainer fitted with a damp cheesecloth.

Combine the milk and cream in a medium saucepan and bring just to a boil over medium-high heat, stirring a few times during the cooking process, about 10 minutes.

Turn off the heat and stir in the vinegar. Let sit until the milk mixture separates from the whey and forms large curds, about 10 minutes. Gently ladle the ricotta mixture through the cheesecloth to strain out the liquid.

Transfer the ricotta from the cheesecloth to a resealable airtight container and stir in salt to taste—start with ¼ teaspoon salt and then add more as needed after stir-and-taste session. Discard the whey. Let sit and cool to room temperature, then refrigerate in the container for up to 1 week. Once you have the recipe down and feel like you've gotten the hang of it, try making variations of the ricotta by stirring in some mix-ins such as honey; fresh herbs and/or lemon or orange zest; or cracked black pepper and a few tablespoons of grated Parmigiano-Reggiano cheese. Any of these would taste excellent on a cracker or even solo, by the spoonful.

PISTACHIO, STRAWBERRY, LEMON, AND RICOTTA GELATO

MAKES ABOUT 1 QUART | ACTIVE TIME: 25 MINUTES | TOTAL TIME: 4 HOURS 25 MINUTES

I first had ricotta gelato years ago in Italy after a day of walking in the hot sun. The rich flavor and cool, velvety texture were like nothing I'd ever tried, and remained fixed in my memory. So a few years ago, I decided to try my hand at a version for one of my cooking classes. The students were amazed by how easy this recipe comes together, mostly because without eggs there's no need to temper the yolks. For sweetness, color, and crunch I've added a bright red swirl of ripe strawberries and chopped salted pistachios.

2 cups ripe strawberries, hulled

1 cup sugar, divided

2 tablespoons fresh lemon juice

2 cups whole milk ricotta

1 cup heavy cream

1 teaspoon pure vanilla extract

¼ cup fresh lemon zest

½ cup roasted salted pistachios, coarsely chopped

Combine the strawberries, ½ cup of the sugar, and the lemon juice in a medium saucepan and bring to a simmer over medium heat. Continue to cook until the strawberries are very soft, about 5 minutes. Use a potato masher to mash the strawberries.

Raise the heat to high, bring to a boil, and continue to cook, stirring occasionally, until the mixture has thickened and reduced by more than half, about 7 more minutes. Transfer to a small bowl placed inside a larger bowl filled with ice water and stir until cooled.

Meanwhile, place the ricotta, cream, remaining ½ cup sugar, the vanilla, and lemon zest in the bowl of a food processor and process until very smooth.

Pour the mixture in the bowl of an ice cream maker and freeze according to the machine's directions. Transfer to a freezer-safe container. Stir the pistachios into the gelato using a large spoon until dispersed evenly throughout, then use a rubber spatula to gently swirl in the strawberry mixture, leaving a red ripple (to avoid turning the mixture pink, do not over-swirl). Return the gelato to the freezer to freeze until firm, about 3 hours. Store the gelato in the freezer for up to 1 week.

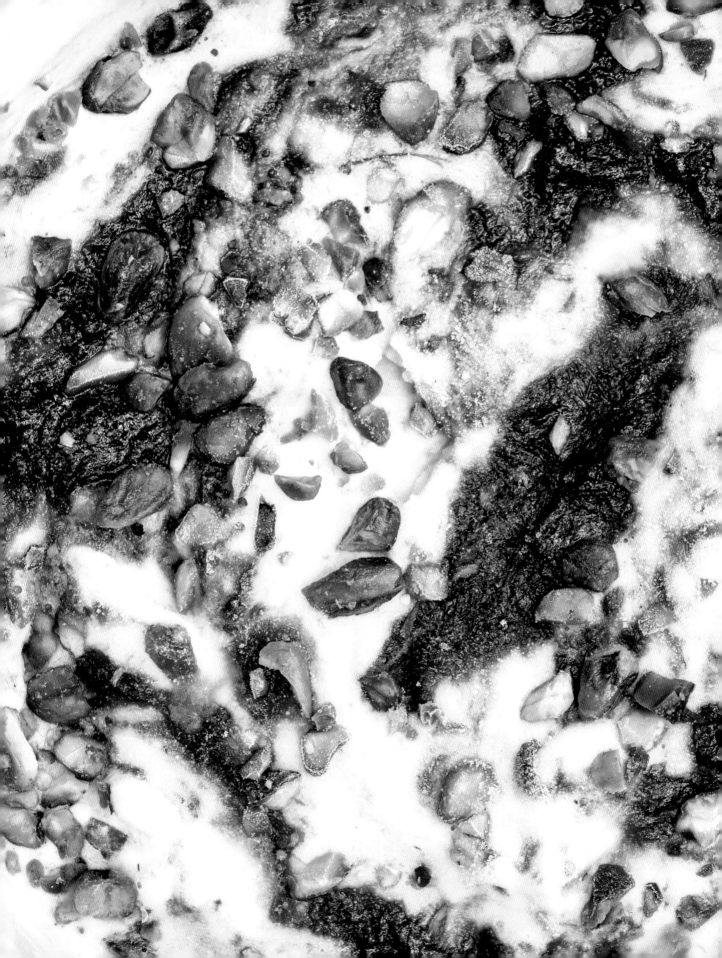

SUMMER CORN ICE CREAM

MAKES ABOUT 1 QUART | ACTIVE TIME: 40 MINUTES | TOTAL TIME: 4 HOURS 40 MINUTES

Corn ice cream may sound unusual, but if you enjoy fresh corn on the cob with butter (or creamed corn), you're in for a treat. The trick in this recipe lies in the process of making the custard; boiling the corncobs acts similarly to making a soup stock, helping to distill and capture the essence of the intense corn flavor that the corn enthusiast seeks. Word to the wise: corn is highly seasonal, and the six- to eight-week stretch from mid-July through early September is corn's sweet spot, as it were. This recipe will taste good regardless, but if you happen to catch the good stuff during that peak season window, the results will leave you grinning from ear to ear.

Note: That niblet of corny humor is a shout-out to my late father-in-law, on whose back deck I was first introduced to the joys of same-day, local New England farm stand corn on the cob. The meal was simple—hot dogs or barbecued chicken, I think—plus a big steaming platter of fresh local corn. As a native Californian, I'd never tasted anything like the intense flavor and candy-like sweetness.

4 ears corn, husks and silk removed

3 cups heavy cream

1 cup whole milk

6 large egg yolks

½ cup light brown sugar

¼ cup granulated sugar

1¼ teaspoons sea salt

Use a sharp knife to remove all the corn kernels from the cob, reserving the cobs. You should have about 3½ cups kernels. Place the kernels in the bowl of a high-powered blender or food processor. Set aside.

Place the cobs in a medium saucepan along with the heavy cream. Bring to a simmer over medium heat, stirring once or twice, about 20 minutes, and cook until the cream has the slightest corn flavor, about 10 more minutes.

Meanwhile, add the milk to the kernels in the blender and blend until smooth, about 1 minute.

Press the corn kernel mixture through a fine-mesh strainer over the cream with the cobs and stir to combine.

In a medium bowl, whisk the egg yolks with both sugars until light golden yellow, about 2 minutes. Discard the cobs, then slowly ladle the hot cream mixture into the egg yolks a bit at a time while whisking constantly until the egg yolk mixture is hot, being careful not to curdle the eggs.

Pour the cream and egg mixture back into the saucepan and cook over medium heat, stirring constantly, until the custard is thick enough just to lightly coat the spoon, about 4 minutes. The custard will be on the thin side, but if you take the spoon out of the custard and run your finger down the middle, it should leave a bare stripe. Stir in the salt.

Transfer the custard back to the medium bowl and place over a large bowl filled with ice water. Stir constantly until the custard is room temperature, then transfer to the refrigerator until cold.

Run the mixture through an ice cream machine according to the machine's instructions. Transfer to a freezer-safe container and freeze until firm, about 3 hours. Store the ice cream in the freezer-safe container in the freezer for up to 1 week.

GINGER, CARDAMOM, AND SAFFRON ICE CREAM

MAKES ABOUT 1 QUART | ACTIVE TIME: 15 MINUTES | TOTAL TIME: 5 HOURS

The popular South Asian creamy frozen dessert *kulfi* inspired this recipe. Denser and creamier than ice cream, kulfi is usually made by boiling down sweetened milk mixed with various flavors (mango, pistachio, rose, ginger, and saffron being among the most popular). The doctored milk is reduced, with constant stirring to prevent burning, until its volume has significantly decreased. Over the course of this process the mixture will take on a caramelized flavor and thicker texture. Finally, it's frozen in kulfi molds until solid.

This ice cream recipe uses flavors that would not be unusual to find in kulfi—fresh ginger, chopped crystalized ginger, cardamom, and saffron, the last of which adds a lovely soft yellow hue as well as a subtle earthiness. Unlike its Eastern cousin, however, my version gets churned in an ice cream machine, then frozen and scooped. The good news is, instead of needing to boil down milk for hours, as kulfi would require, this recipe starts with canned sweetened condensed milk, evaporated milk, and heavy cream to enable cooking time to be significantly cut down. Before you know it you'll end up with exotic, kulfi-like ice cream—super creamy, spice-filled, and delicious!

Note: I've recommended Australian crystalized ginger here if you can locate it because its creamy texture is particularly well-suited to ice cream. Look for it and the other spices at specialty food stores.

1 (12-ounce) can evaporated milk

1 teaspoon saffron threads

4 cardamom pods

2 tablespoons grated fresh ginger

1 cup heavy cream

1 (14-ounce) can sweetened condensed milk

¼ teaspoon sea salt

⅔ cup chopped crystalized ginger (preferably Australian, if you can find it)

Place the evaporated milk, saffron, cardamom, and grated ginger in a small saucepan. Stir to combine. Bring to a boil over medium heat (it should take about 4 minutes), then turn off the heat. Let sit until the mixture smells very fragrant, about 10 minutes. Set aside.

In a medium bowl, whisk to combine the heavy cream and sweetened condensed milk. Pour the hot evaporated milk mixture through a fine-mesh strainer over the cream mixture. Stir in the salt and refrigerate until cold.

Pour the mixture into the bowl of an ice cream maker and freeze according to the machine's directions.

Stir in the crystallized ginger, transfer to a freezer-safe container, and freeze until firm, 3 to 4 hours. The ice cream can be stored in the freezer for up to 1 week.

WHITE ALMOND SORBET

MAKES ABOUT 1 QUART | ACTIVE TIME: 10 MINUTES | TOTAL TIME: 4 HOURS 20 MINUTES

Did you know that there's a difference between sorbet and sherbet? If so, one point. If you knew what the difference actually *is* (sorbet contains no dairy, whereas sherbet contains a little milk or cream, giving it a creamier texture), two points.

In case you are wondering which is a better bet—*sor*-bet or *sher*-bet—this recipe, inspired by those Italian almond granitas often served with Italian breakfast buffets, splits the difference. Technically it's a sorbet—no dairy—yet it has the characteristic creamy texture of a sherbet from the inclusion of almond milk. It does require an ice cream machine to churn.

Sweet, creamy, and superbly refreshing, I love doing what the Italians do and serving some alongside breakfast. It's also good after lunch, after dinner, or anytime in between on a hot and sultry day.

1¼ cups water

1¼ cups sugar

2 cups cold unsweetened almond milk

1 teaspoon pure almond extract

In a medium saucepan, combine the water and sugar and bring to boil over high heat, about 3 minutes. Stir until the sugar is dissolved, about 3 minutes, then pour into a large measuring cup or pitcher and refrigerate until very cold.

Stir the almond milk and almond extract into the sugar syrup until combined.

Run the mixture through an ice cream machine according to the machine's instructions, then transfer to a freezer-safe container and freeze until completely frozen, 3 to 4 hours. Store the sorbet in the freezer for up to 1 week.

RED GRAPEFRUIT–ROSE SORBET

MAKES ABOUT 1 QUART | ACTIVE TIME: 20 MINUTES | TOTAL TIME: 5 HOURS 20 MINUTES

Rosewater, a popular flavor found in many Middle Eastern dishes and desserts, is made—no surprise—by steeping rose petals in water. Its potent flavor should be used judiciously, but in moderation provides a welcome and unexpected exotic dimension to many dishes. I like rosewater with grapefruit—the bright, summery flavors complement (and can stand up to) each other. Wine adds complexity and depth and continues the rosy theme. The grapefruit peel performs double duty, first cooked along with the other ingredients to draw out the lovely, tart citrus oils, then strained out and (while the mixture freezes) thinly sliced and coated in sugar to create a crunchy candied topping.

1½ cups sugar, divided

1½ cups dry rosé wine

Fresh peel (peeled using a vegetable peeler) from 1 whole ruby red grapefruit

1½ cups fresh unstrained ruby red grapefruit juice

2 tablespoons rosewater

Combine 1 cup of the sugar, the wine, and grapefruit peel in a medium saucepan. Bring to a boil over medium-high heat, about 6 minutes, and continue to cook until the alcohol scent subsides, about 4 more minutes. Transfer the mixture to a large pitcher or medium bowl and refrigerate until cold, about 1 hour.

Strain the mixture through a fine-mesh strainer over a large pitcher or another bowl. Reserve the grapefruit peel and set aside.

Stir in the grapefruit juice and rosewater. At this point, if desired, the mixture can be stored in an airtight container in the refrigerator for up to 1 day.

Run the mixture through an ice cream machine according to the machine's instructions. Transfer the sorbet to a freezer-safe container and freeze until solid, 3 to 4 hours.

Meanwhile, pour the remaining ½ cup sugar into a small bowl. Thinly slice the reserved grapefruit peel and toss in the sugar to coat. Transfer to a parchment paper–lined plate to dry, about 2 hours. The candied grapefruit peel can be stored in an airtight container at room temperature for up to 1 week.

Serve the sorbet topped with the candied grapefruit. The sorbet can be stored in the freezer for up to 1 week.

RIPE MELON SORBET

MAKES ABOUT 1 QUART | ACTIVE TIME: 12 MINUTES | TOTAL TIME: 4½ HOURS

Melon is one of the few fruits I'm a stickler about waiting until peak season to eat. After I started buying melons at the farmers market years ago, I realized that there's just no substitute for the real, in-season deal—i.e., melons that are ripe and heavy with juice, bright-colored, fragrant, and sweet. Knowing whether a melon is ripe depends on the specific melon—tips by melon can be researched online—but the easiest way is simply to purchase it at the farmers market, where, by definition, you know that it will be in season. Once I realized this, I decided there was just no point in eating off-season melons, whether in sliced wedges or fruit salad cubes (for more hot takes on melon, see page 57). In short, your principal criteria should be which melon is freshest and in season. Regardless of the type, this recipe will allow each melon's individual fragrance and flavor to come through, and hopefully encourage you to experiment and try a range of melon options.

1 cup sugar

1 cup water

4 cups chopped honeydew, cantaloupe, canary, or other ripe melon

2 tablespoons fresh lemon juice

In a medium saucepan, combine the sugar and water and bring to boil over high heat, about 3 minutes. Stir until the sugar is dissolved, about 3 minutes, then pour the syrup into a large measuring cup or pitcher and refrigerate until very cold, about 30 minutes.

Combine the melon, sugar syrup, and lemon juice in a high-powered blender and blend on high speed until very smooth.

Run the mixture through an ice cream machine according to the machine's instructions. Transfer to a freezer-safe container and freeze until solid, 3 to 4 hours. The sorbet can be stored in the freezer for up to 1 week.

WATERMELON-LIME POPS WITH CHILE SALT

MAKES 8 | ACTIVE TIME: 10 MINUTES | TOTAL TIME: 8 HOURS 10 MINUTES

Taking a field trip to downtown LA's Olvera Street was an annual school tradition when I was growing up. Designed to recreate old Los Angeles, the narrow, tree-lined street is in effect a Mexican marketplace filled with restaurants, shops, and vendors selling everything from *taquitos* to Day of the Dead *nicho* boxes featuring groups of skeletons happily dancing, making music, playing *futbol*, and so forth. Invariably, upon arrival my friends and I would make a beeline for our favorite vendor, who simply sold fresh, cold, ripe fruit on a stick. The idea was to sprinkle the fruit with (or dip it into) the various toppings arrayed on the shelf attached to his stall; these included hot sauce, salt, chile powder, and more. It might sound strange to the uninitiated, but fruit, salt, and chile are a perfect match. (If you're a cautious or risk-averse eater, it may help to think of salt as more than just salty and chile powder as more than just spicy; both actually act as flavor enhancers that elevate the natural sweetness of the fruits.) These Olvera Street–inspired ice pops harness this phenomenon, using a chile-salt mixture or Tajín seasoning (a popular blend of chiles, salt, and dehydrated lime juice) to jumpstart the watermelon flavor. If using the Tajín, reduce the salt to ½ teaspoon, omitting the 1½ teaspoons salt for dipping the pops into.

4 cups chopped seedless watermelon

2 tablespoons fresh lime zest

⅓ cup fresh lime juice

¾ cup sugar

2 teaspoons Himalayan pink salt, divided

2 tablespoons Aleppo chile flakes or Tajín (see headnote)

Combine the watermelon, lime zest, lime juice, sugar, and ½ teaspoon of the salt in a blender and blend on high speed until the mixture is smooth, about 2 minutes.

Pour the mixture evenly into eight ⅓-cup ice pop molds.

Freeze until the mixture is a slushy-like consistency, 2 to 3 hours. Remove from the freezer and insert a wooden ice pop stick into each pop. Return to the freezer and freeze until solid, about 6 hours or overnight.

On a small plate, mix together the remaining 1½ teaspoons salt and the Aleppo chile or spread out the Tajín. Remove the pops from the molds and dip each pop in the seasoning mixture. Serve immediately.

FREEZING FRUIT

Frozen fruit makes for a great staple freezer pantry item that can be added to smoothies, alcoholic drinks, blended with a bit of fruit juice, water, simple syrup, or alcohol for an easy dessert, or simply snacked on when it's boiling out. Try frozen grapes, stone fruit, bananas, or ripe, frozen berries dipped in honeyed yogurt or melted chocolate. You'll note that frozen fruit is used throughout this book, such as in the Papaya, Ginger, and Lime Smoothie (page 17), Mock Vanilla Milkshake (page 12), Berry Stew with Sweetened Crème Fraîche (page 180), all three shrubs (pages 189, 191, and 192), and the White Grape and Elderflower Boozy Slushie (page 203). With respect to blended smoothies and drinks, frozen fruit has the virtue of providing flavor while cooling them, unlike ice, which cools but dilutes.

The only downside is that frozen fruit can't really stand in for fresh (in a salad, for example), since it tends to lose its fresh snap and firm texture after thawing. But it can be used quite successfully in the applications listed above. Yes, you can also buy pre-frozen fruit, but doing it yourself is easy, cheap, and helps preserve fruit on the verge of going bad (looking at you, bananas) as well as fruit that is at peak ripeness—and it allows for options you wouldn't see in the frozen fruit case at the supermarket.

To freeze fruit: Line a small baking pan with parchment paper and layer on the fruit (which has been rinsed and dried), leaving a bit of space in between each piece. Freeze until solid, 3 to 6 hours depending on the type of fruit or vegetable, then transfer to an airtight container. Write the date on the container so that you know when you froze it. If stored correctly, the fruit will last up to 4 months in the freezer.

CHAMOMILE, STRAWBERRY, AND NECTARINE PALETAS

MAKES 10 | ACTIVE TIME: 10 MINUTES | TOTAL TIME: 5 HOURS 10 MINUTES

As an LA kid, frozen treats on a hot day didn't mean soft serve, Italian ice, or red, white, and blue rocket pops. Instead, we'd head for the local bodega or market and pick out a selection of *paletas*—naturally sweetened (usually) Mexican ice pops. These came in a wide variety, from your basic 101-level flavors (strawberry, banana, lemon) to your more advanced ones (tamarind, horchata, blood orange). I missed paletas after leaving LA, but later in life I discovered that making them from scratch is a cinch. This recipe originally came about when I accidentally made too much iced chamomile tea and needed to do something with the surplus. Happily, my hunch paid off: the chopped fresh strawberries and nectarine and mild and sweet chamomile flavor fit each other to a tea (for further material of this caliber, keep your eye out for my upcoming late-night streaming comedy special).

1 lemon

2½ cups water

¾ cup sugar

⅛ ounce loose-leaf chamomile tea
(about 2 tablespoons or 4 tea bags)

1 cup sliced ripe strawberries

1 ripe nectarine, pitted and thinly sliced

Use a vegetable peeler to peel the skin off the lemon, leaving the white pith. Then slice the lemon in half crosswise and juice the lemon. Reserve 3 tablespoons juice and set aside.

In a small saucepan, bring the water, sugar, and lemon peel just to a boil over high heat, about 4 minutes. Turn off the heat add the tea bags. Transfer to a large measuring cup or pitcher and refrigerate until cold, about 1 hour.

Once cold, remove the tea mixture from the refrigerator and stir in the lemon juice, then pour the mixture through a fine-mesh strainer into another spouted container. Set aside.

Divide the strawberries and nectarine evenly among 10 ice pop molds. Then pour the tea mixture over the top of each and top with an ice pop stick. Freeze for at least 4 hours or overnight. Unmold and serve. The paletas can be stored in the molds in the freezer for up to 1 week.

BANANA AND ALMOND MILK PALETAS DIPPED IN DARK CHOCOLATE

MAKES 10 | ACTIVE TIME: 25 MINUTES | TOTAL TIME: 8 HOURS

I borrowed the idea of freezing leftover smoothies into ice pops from my Aunt Gail. To me, the approach to leftovers seemed both innovative and delicious. These are vegan, incidentally, but also accidentally—I was trying to create a hot-weather-appropriate dessert that was creamy yet light (double-check that your dark chocolate doesn't contain milk). As with all homemade ice pops, paletas or others, they take a while to freeze. But the delightful final product is worth the wait.

5 ripe bananas, peeled

¾ cup confectioners' sugar

¼ cup almond flour

½ teaspoon sea salt

½ teaspoon ground cinnamon

¼ teaspoon freshly grated nutmeg

½ teaspoon pure almond extract

1 cup almond milk

1½ cups chopped dark chocolate

½ cup coarsely chopped toasted or raw almonds for sprinkling

Place the bananas in the bowl of a high-powered blender or food processor along with the confectioners' sugar, almond flour, salt, cinnamon, nutmeg, almond extract, and almond milk and blend until smooth.

Pour the mixture evenly into 10 ice pop molds (about 6 tablespoons each) and freeze until firm, about 6 hours (or overnight). The paletas can be kept in the pop molds in the freezer at this stage for up to 1 week.

Line a baking sheet with parchment paper and place in the freezer. After the paletas are completely frozen, unmold them and place on the parchment paper to refreeze, about 20 minutes.

Meanwhile, place the chocolate in a double boiler over medium-high heat, stirring occasionally until just melted, about 3 minutes. Alternatively, place the chocolate in a microwave-safe bowl and melt on high in 30-second increments, stirring in between, until almost completely melted, about 1½ minutes. Remove from the microwave and stir until smooth. Let cool slightly.

Working fast, hold each paleta, one at a time, over the bowl of chocolate and use a spoon to drizzle the chocolate over the top of the paletas. Place back on the parchment-lined baking sheet and sprinkle with the almonds. Return to the freezer until firm, about 10 minutes. Serve.

Once dipped in the chocolate, the paletas can be stored in the freezer wrapped in plastic and placed on the parchment-lined baking sheet for up to 1 week.

MALTED CHOCOLATE ICEBOX CAKE

MAKES 1 (8-INCH) CAKE | ACTIVE TIME: 30 MINUTES | TOTAL TIME: 4½ HOURS

I absolutely love the concept behind the icebox cake. I'd define an icebox cake as an oven-free cake you can throw together on the stovetop, or with zero cooking, that is nonetheless attractive enough to bring over to a friend's party. The name derives from the fact that these cakes are typically allowed to soften for several hours—or better yet overnight—in the icebox (or, in the last ninety years or so, the fridge), thus allowing the ingredients to comingle flavors and exchange business cards.

The different versions of the icebox cake are many. Some are made in a pie tin, others molded into baking tins. This particular one, which I think of as "soda shop meets vintage/retro," is actually freeform (i.e., can be hand-assembled on a plate), not to mention totally oven-less. Its primary building block is none other than the Nabisco classic chocolate wafer cookie. While I don't often advocate for store-bought cookies, these not-too-sweet dark chocolate wafers perform yeoman's work for this cake, serving as the perfect brick. The result is a stable, voluminous structure, held together by the ricotta-chocolate malt "mortar." Layers of chocolate malted ricotta crème, sandwiched between crispy chocolate wafers and crushed chocolate malted candies . . . this cake takes the icebox cake!

Double points if you make your own ricotta for this recipe (see page 157).

2 cups (about 8 ounces) chocolate-covered malt ball candies, plus 16 more for garnish

2 cups whole milk ricotta (see headnote)

⅓ cup Dutch-process cocoa powder

1 cup malted milk powder

2 tablespoons honey

½ teaspoon sea salt

2 cups heavy cream

49 store-bought round, flat chocolate wafer cookies (from two 9-ounce packages)

recipe continues on page 174

Place the 2 cups malt balls in a food processor and pulse until finely chopped (about 30 times). Transfer to a medium bowl. No need to wipe out the food processor bowl.

Combine the ricotta, cocoa powder, malted milk powder, honey, and salt in the food processor. Process until the mixture is very smooth, about 2 minutes.

In the bowl of an electric mixer, beat the cream until stiff peaks form, about 2 minutes. Fold the ricotta-chocolate mixture into the whipped cream. Set aside.

To form the bottom layer of the cake, place 6 cookies on a plate or cake stand, to form a 7¾-inch-diameter circle. Add one more cookie to the center to finish forming the first layer. There will be gaps between the cookies.

Spoon 1 cup ricotta mixture onto the center of the circle of cookies. Use an offset spatula or rubber spatula to evenly and gently spread the layer of ricotta mixture, leaving a little of the cookies on the outer edge exposed. (Note: The first layer is a bit tricky . . . if necessary, place a little dollop of the cream mixture under each cookie to help hold them in place or use fingers to gently hold the cookies in place while spreading the ricotta mixture.) Once the layer is complete, sprinkle with 2 tablespoons chopped candies.

Repeat this process, gently adding the remaining cookies, ricotta mixture, and candies and ending with the ricotta being the top layer. In all, you should have 7 layers of cookies and 7 layers of the ricotta mixture. Use an offset spatula to smooth the top layer of the ricotta mixture and sprinkle all over the top with more chopped candy.

Decorate the edge of the top of the cake with whole malted milk balls. Transfer the cake to the refrigerator and leave uncovered until the cookies have softened and the cake is easy to slice, about 4 hours or overnight. The cake can be made up to 1 day ahead of time.

SALTED LEMON SEMIFREDDO

MAKES 1 (9-INCH) ROUND SEMIFREDDO | ACTIVE TIME: 45 MINUTES | TOTAL TIME: 8 HOURS 45 MINUTES

Think of it as ice cream you slice like a cake. Made from lemon custard folded with mascarpone and cream, then finished with whipped cream and lemon zest, this cool and airy frozen mousse conjures the Italian Riviera. When making the Quick and Spicy Mediterranean Lemon Pickles (page 217), leave out the chiles and oregano.

For the semifreddo

1½ cups heavy cream

½ cup mascarpone cheese

8 large egg yolks

1½ cups sugar

¾ cup fresh lemon juice (from about 9 lemons)

2 teaspoons brine from Quick and Spicy Mediterranean Lemon Pickles (page 217, see headnote)

¼ cup finely chopped rind from Quick and Spicy Mediterranean Lemon Pickles (page 217, see headnote), pith and flesh discarded

Fresh lemon zest for serving

For the topping

1 cup heavy cream

¼ cup confectioners' sugar

To make the semifreddo

Line a 9-inch-diameter by 2½-inch-tall round cake pan with plastic wrap, leaving a 2-inch overhang. Set aside.

Using a stand mixer or a hand mixer in a large bowl, whisk the heavy cream and mascarpone on low

speed until smooth, then increase the mixer speed to medium-high and beat until stiff peaks form, about 2 minutes. Transfer to a medium bowl and refrigerate. Clean the bowl to reuse for the next step.

Combine the egg yolks, sugar, lemon juice, and brine in the large mixer bowl set over a small saucepan of boiling water not touching the water. Hold the bowl in place using a dishcloth to protect your hand while whisking constantly with the other hand until the mixture is very hot to the touch and foamy and/or a candy thermometer reads 165°F, 4 to 8 minutes. Take off the heat, then transfer to an electric mixer and beat on high speed until the mixture has cooled and is light and fluffy, 15 to 20 minutes.

Stir the chopped rind into the lemon custard, then fold in the whipped cream mixture until all is combined. Transfer to the prepared cake pan. Cover with the overhang of plastic wrap and freeze until firm, about 8 hours or overnight. At this point, the semifreddo can be stored in the freezer, wrapped in the plastic wrap, for up to 3 days.

To serve, unwrap the plastic wrap from the top of the pan and invert the semifreddo onto a large plate, peeling off the rest of the plastic wrap. Transfer back to the freezer while making the whipped cream topping.

To make the topping

In a large mixer bowl, whisk the heavy cream and confectioners' sugar on medium-high speed until soft peaks form, about 2 minutes.

Top the semifreddo with the whipped cream and lemon zest. Serve immediately.

COCONUT RICE PUDDING WITH FRESH BERRIES AND MANGO

SERVES 4 TO 6 | ACTIVE TIME: 30 MINUTES | TOTAL TIME: 2½ HOURS

This recipe is loosely inspired by sticky rice with mango, a classic Thai dessert that is a personal favorite of mine on account of its slightly stodgy, sweet, refreshing, and coconut-y properties. (If you've never tried it, I recommend making it a priority to do so on your next pad thai run.) Hot-weather appropriate, gluten-free, and dairy-free, it's fusion cuisine of sorts—a translation of the Thai dessert to a Western concept, built around coconut milk and jasmine rice. This rice goes through a series of steps resembling a deluxe spa treatment, being first toasted in coconut oil; then cooked in coconut milk; next, infused with fresh ginger and sweetened condensed milk; and, finally, cooled down, provided a luxurious mango-berry treatment, and massaged with hot, eucalyptus-scented stones (OK, I made that last step up). Since a bit of stove time is required, consider making it either early in the morning or at night when temps are cooler.

¾ cup jasmine rice

2 tablespoons virgin (unrefined) coconut oil

3 cups whole coconut milk from 2 (13.5-ounce) cans

½ cup sweetened condensed milk

1 teaspoon grated fresh ginger

¼ teaspoon sea salt

1 cup hulled and quartered strawberries

1 cup raspberries

1 ripe mango, peeled, pitted, and chopped

Rinse and drain the rice until the water runs clear. Set aside.

Warm the coconut oil in a medium saucepan over medium-high heat. Add the rice and cook, stirring occasionally, until lightly toasted, 2 to 3 minutes. Stir in the coconut milk and bring to a full boil, 2 to 3 minutes. Reduce the heat to medium and continue to cook, stirring occasionally to prevent the rice from sticking to the pan, until the mixture is thickened and the rice is tender, about 18 minutes.

Turn off the heat. Stir in the sweetened condensed milk, ginger, and salt. Transfer to a bowl to cool slightly, about 20 minutes, then refrigerate for at least 2 hours, or until ready to serve.

To serve, divide among serving dishes and top with the strawberries, raspberries and mango.

TROPICAL CRISPY BARS

MAKES 12 | ACTIVE TIME: 25 MINUTES | TOTAL TIME: 1 HOUR 5 MINUTES

The premise to these addictively chewy bars is "classic crispy rice treat goes to Hawaii." To achieve the full luau effect, nutty browned butter, vanilla, and a bit of unrefined coconut oil flavor the melted marshmallows, while macadamia nuts, freeze-dried pineapple, and coconut chips take the crunchy cereal part all the way to the islands. If you're serving these on a hot day, maybe skip the white chocolate glaze, lest a sticky-sweet lava flow ruin your guests' resort wear.

Cooking spray for the pan

4 cups puffed rice cereal, such as Rice Krispies

1½ cups roughly chopped roasted and salted macadamia nuts, divided

1½ cups toasted unsalted coconut chips, divided

1½ cups freeze-dried pineapple pieces, chopped into ½-inch pieces if large, divided

6 tablespoons salted butter

2 tablespoons virgin (unrefined) coconut oil

1 teaspoon pure vanilla extract

6 cups mini marshmallows

2 ounces good-quality white chocolate chopped (about ½ cup) and melted (see headnote)

Spray a 9 by 13-inch baking pan (ideally a metal cake pan with 2-inch-high sides) with cooking spray and set aside.

In a large bowl, mix together the cereal, 1 cup of the macadamia nuts, 1 cup of the coconut chips, and 1 cup of the pineapple pieces. Set aside.

Melt the butter in a large saucepan over medium heat and cook, swirling the pan constantly, until the butter begins to smell nutty and turn light brown, 9 to 11 minutes.

Add the coconut oil, vanilla, and marshmallows and stir to combine. Cook, stirring occasionally, until the marshmallows are completely melted, 2 to 3 minutes. Turn off the heat.

Stir the cereal mixture into the marshmallow mixture until evenly combined.

Transfer the cereal mixture to the prepared pan and use a large spoon or spatula to gently spread it out evenly. Sprinkle the remaining ½ cup macadamia nuts, coconut chips, and pineapple over the top and use your hands to gently press into the cereal mixture. Let sit at room temperature until set, about 30 minutes.

If not too hot out (see headnote), drizzle with melted white chocolate. Refrigerate until the chocolate solidifies, about 10 minutes.

Cut evenly into 12 squares. The crispy bars can be stored in an airtight container at room temperature for up to 3 days.

BERRY STEW WITH SWEETENED CRÈME FRAÎCHE

SERVES 4 | ACTIVE TIME: 15 MINUTES | TOTAL TIME: 1 HOUR 15 MINUTES

On the surface, I realize, the word *stew* suggests neither dessert nor hot weather food. But hopefully this chilled dessert, loaded with fresh berries and fragrant herbs, will force you to reexamine your preconceived stew notions. This recipe's mixture of berries with an herb-infused simple syrup, served with lightly sweetened vanilla-scented crème fraîche, is refreshing, sweet, tart, and creamy all rolled into one—something like a crust-free pie but with herbal and woodsy notes that add depth and interest. My herb of choice here is lemon thyme, a variety of thyme heavily perfumed with notes of citrus, as the name implies. It can be found at the farmers market, specialty grocery stores, or gardening center, but if you're having difficulty locating it, feel free to use regular thyme. (Either way, keep in mind that eating this dessert will be a bit thyme-consuming.)

2 cups strawberries, hulled, halved, or quartered if large

1 cup blackberries

1 cup blueberries

1 cup raspberries

¾ cup plus 2 tablespoons sugar, divided

8 sprigs fresh lemon thyme or regular thyme

5 sprigs fresh mint

Peel from 1 whole lemon

1¼ cups water

1 cup crème fraîche

2 teaspoons pure vanilla extract

Place the strawberries, blackberries, blueberries, and raspberries in the bottom of a large bowl. Set aside.

Combine ¾ cup of the sugar, the lemon thyme, mint, and lemon peel in a small saucepan along with the water. Bring to a simmer over medium heat and continue to cook, stirring once or twice, until the sugar has dissolved and the mixture smells very fragrant, about 12 minutes total.

Pour the hot liquid through a fine-mesh strainer over the berries and stir to combine.

Use a meat mallet or potato masher to mash the berries, leaving some intact and some completely mashed. Cover and refrigerate until cold, about 1 hour. At this point, the berry stew can be stored in an airtight container for up to 2 days in the refrigerator, if desired.

Meanwhile, in a small bowl, whisk together the crème fraîche, remaining 2 tablespoons sugar, and the vanilla. This can be made up to 2 days ahead of time and stored in an airtight container in the refrigerator.

Divide the berry stew among 4 bowls and top each with a dollop of the sweetened crème fraîche. Serve immediately.

DRINKS

MELON AND LIME AGUA FRESCA

SERVES 4 TO 6 | ACTIVE TIME: 15 MINUTES | TOTAL TIME: 15 MINUTES

Agua fresca, a sweet, non-carbonated drink popular in Mexico, translates to "fresh water"—and it lives up to this name nicely, thanks to its thirst-quenching properties. Somewhat reminiscent of lemonade, agua fresca comes in a variety of flavors, being made with a combination of fruits, flowers, and sometimes even seeds and pods. Some variations are dusted with chile powder. In this particular variation, the sweet floral flavor of melon costars with bright citrus notes of lime, resulting in a lovely, light green nonalcoholic concoction you'll wish you could dive into on a humid day.

7 cups chopped ripe green melon, such as honeydew, honey globe, or bailan, from 1 large melon

¾ cup sugar

1 tablespoon fresh lime zest

¾ cup fresh lime juice

4 cups water

Lime wedges for garnish

Place the melon, sugar, lime zest, and lime juice in a blender and blend until smooth.

Use a rubber spatula to push the melon mixture through a fine-mesh strainer into the bottom of a large pitcher or bowl. You should have about 3 cups melon juice mixture. Discard any remaining pulp. Add the water to the melon juice and stir to combine. Refrigerate until ready to serve.

To serve, fill glasses with ice, then ladle the agua fresca over the top. Garnish with lime wedges. Serve immediately or store in a large pitcher in the refrigerator for up to 2 days (garnish just before serving). Stir a few times before serving.

HIBISCUS, ROSE HIP, AND BERRY AGUA FRESCA

SERVES 4 TO 6 | ACTIVE TIME: 8 MINUTES | TOTAL TIME: 1½ HOURS

This sweet, tart, refreshingly fragrant *agua fresca* supplements the flavors of blueberries and strawberries with floral notes, imparted by the hibiscus petal and rose hip tea. The edible hibiscus is a plant found in subtropical and tropical locations known for its vibrant flowers, with petals that get plucked, dried, and steeped in water, resulting in a tartly flavored, magenta-colored tea. Apparently, Egyptians used hibiscus tea for millennia (including the pharaohs—no joke) as a cure for health woes and—more germane here—to lower their body temperatures. If it worked for the likes of Tutankhamun, Raamses, and Amenhotep, you won't find me casting doubts. As for rose hips, you've likely seen them growing alongside the dunes if you've ever been to Cape Cod. The seeded fruit of roses, rose hips are chunky, reddish orange berries with a sour tartness that is frequently harnessed for use in jams, syrups, and teas. What with its hibiscus, rosehips, and berries, this agua fresca is chockablock with vitamin C—a good thing, since that particular nutrient gets sweated out in the heat. Conversely, vitamin C from a suitable source may help speed recovery after heat exposure from exercise—participating in a camel race, say, or putting out an oil rig fire. Or simply living everyday life during summer in the city.

1 ounce dried rosehips

2 ounces loose-leaf hibiscus flower tea

5 cups water, divided

⅔ cup sugar

2 cups strawberries, hulled, plus more for serving

2 cups blueberries, plus more for serving

Place the rosehips and hibiscus flowers in a small saucepan along with 4 cups of the water and bring to a boil. Turn off the heat and let steep for 20 minutes.

Place the sugar, strawberries, blueberries, and remaining 1 cup water in a blender. Blend until smooth.

Pour the berry mixture through a fine-mesh strainer into the bottom of a large pitcher or bowl, then pour the hibiscus-rosehip mixture over the top through the fine-mesh strainer onto the berry mixture. Stir to combine, then refrigerate until cold, about 1 hour.

To serve, fill glasses with ice, then ladle the agua fresca over the top. Garnish with fresh berries. Serve immediately or store in a large pitcher in the refrigerator for up to 2 days (garnish just before serving). Stir a few times before serving.

TAMARIND AND CHILE AGUA FRESCA

SERVES 4 TO 6 | ACTIVE TIME: 15 MINUTES | TOTAL TIME: 1 HOUR 25 MINUTES

The combination may sound odd, but this refreshing *agua fresca* yields a perfect balance of sweet, tangy, salty, and spicy. Inspired by a popular Mexican candy, it's a mixture of tamarind, ancho chile, water, sugar, and lemon juice. Tamarind, the tart brown fruit of a hardwood tree native to Africa, is sold in a few different formats—the simplest to use is a super thick paste, typically sold in blocks with seeds still embedded in the pulp. There are also more processed, seedless versions of tamarind paste (with additional ingredients and flavors), or you can purchase whole, dried tamarind pods, which ultimately taste the freshest but take the most work. This variety ultimately tastes the freshest, though more work is involved to peel and de-string the pods and separate the pulp from the seeds.

20 dried sweet tamarind pods

¾ cup sugar

2 teaspoons ground ancho chile, plus more for rimming the glasses

6½ cups water, divided

½ cup fresh lemon juice, plus more lemon for rimming the glasses

Fine sea salt for rimming the glasses

Peel the outer shells off the tamarind pod and place the pulp-covered seeds in a medium saucepan along with the sugar, ancho chile, and 1 cup of the water. Bring the mixture to a simmer over medium-high heat, about 6 minutes. Reduce the heat to medium-low, cover, and simmer until the tamarind pulp is very soft, 8 to 10 more minutes.

Strain the mixture by using a rubber spatula to get as much of the pulp off of the seeds as you can and push the pulp through a fine-mesh strainer over a large pitcher or measuring cup. Continue to add the remaining water, about 1 cup at a time, to the tamarind mixture in the strainer, while stirring and pushing with the rubber spatula to get as much pulp as possible through the strainer. Discard the large seeds left over.

Stir in the lemon juice and refrigerate until very cold, about 1 hour.

To serve, combine 1 tablespoon salt and 1 tablespoon ancho chile powder in a small flat dish. Rub the lemon around the rim of each serving glass, then dip in the chile and salt mixture. Fill the glasses with ice and pour in the tamarind agua fresca. Serve immediately or store in a large pitcher in the refrigerator for up to 2 days (prep the glasses just before serving). Stir a few times before serving.

GINGER STRAWBERRY SHRUB

MAKES 2¼ CUPS SHRUB CONCENTRATE | ACTIVE TIME: 8 MINUTES | TOTAL TIME: 1 HOUR

For those unfamiliar with the culinary use of the term *shrub*, I am advocating consuming neither a liquefied hedge, bush, briar, nor bramble patch in this recipe. To mixologists, a shrub means a drink made by combining fizzy water with a nonalcoholic syrup comprised of vinegar and fruit concentrates, sweeteners, and/or aromatics. Essentially a modernized version of an old-fashioned tonic, the shrub's pairing of sweet and tart makes for an oddly satisfying and highly refreshing concoction. The vinegar is really the key; first, because it gives the drink its tangy, distinctive bite, and second, because the vinegar's preservative properties help to extend the life of soft, ripe summer fruits on their last legs (or would, in a world where fruit had legs). Shrubs, which have been around since colonial days, incidentally, can be as strong or as subtle as you like, based on how much water you add. I prefer them rather strong and very cold, so I usually use cold filtered or sparkling water and lots of ice. (Unsurprisingly, alcohol, in particular vodka, is a popular addition—but not a required one.) This particular shrub is based on white balsamic infused with fragrant, in-season strawberries and ginger. Give it a chance and see if you don't find it delicious and thirst-quenching.

⅓ cup chopped, peeled fresh ginger

1 cup fresh hulled strawberries, plus more (optional) for garnish

¼ cup water

1¼ cups white balsamic vinegar

1 cup sugar

Ice cubes for serving

Sparkling water for serving

Licorice mint and candied ginger for garnish (optional)

Place the ginger, strawberries, and water in a blender and blend until smooth, about 1 minute. Set aside.

Combine the vinegar and sugar in a small saucepan and bring to a boil over high heat, stirring occasionally.

Pour the strawberry-ginger mixture into the vinegar and stir to combine. Strain the mixture through a fine-mesh strainer over a measuring cup. Transfer to a clean bottle or jar. Refrigerate until cold, 45 minutes to 1 hour.

To serve, pour a little of the shrub into a glass with ice and top with sparkling water. Garnish with fresh strawberries and licorice mint and candied ginger, if desired. Store the shrub in the refrigerator for up to 1 month (top up and garnish just before serving).

BLACKBERRY, UME, SHISO SHRUB

MAKES 2 CUPS SHRUB CONCENTRATE | ACTIVE TIME: 10 MINUTES | TOTAL TIME: 1 HOUR

This blackberry-centric shrub is augmented with *shiso* leaves and *umeboshi* to lend it a Japanese-inspired flavor (both can be found in your local Japanese or Asian market). Shiso (also known as *perilla*) is in the mint family and has its own unique flavor, though basil is a good substitute if you can't find it. The *ume* fruit, from which umeboshi are derived, has a flavor and texture somewhere between a plum and apricot. Umeboshi are dried, salted ume fruits, and their sodium acts as an electrolyte to help regulate hydration and thus prevent overheating (or offering relief if you're already there). Keep in mind: the shrub base has intense flavor and needs to be diluted. My recipe below is topped with sparking water. But, if you feel the urge to top yours off with cold filtered water or prosecco, no objection here.

½ cup purple shiso leaves (if unavailable, substitute green shiso or basil), plus more (optional) for serving

1 cup fresh blackberries, plus more (optional) for serving

2 pitted umeboshi plums, plus more for serving

¼ cup water

1 cup apple cider vinegar

1 cup sugar

Ice cubes

Sparkling water for serving

Place the shiso, blackberries, umeboshi, and water in a blender and blend until the leaves are pulverized, about 30 seconds. Set aside.

Combine the vinegar and sugar in a small saucepan and bring to a boil over high heat, stirring occasionally.

Pour the blackberry mixture into the vinegar and stir to combine, then push the mixture through a fine-mesh strainer over a measuring cup. Transfer to a clean bottle or jar and refrigerate until cold, 45 minutes to 1 hour.

To serve, muddle an umeboshi into the bottom of a tall glass, pour a little of the shrub on top along with ice, and top with sparkling water. Garnish with fresh blackberries and shiso leaves,

PINEAPPLE TURMERIC SHRUB

MAKES 2 CUPS SHRUB CONCENTRATE | ACTIVE TIME: 8 MINUTES | TOTAL TIME: 1 HOUR

Made with sweet pineapple and fresh turmeric, this shrub boasts a sunny yellow color and flavor that will wipe away any hot-and-sweaty blues (setting aside for the moment the fact that yellow and blue make green). It is made in similar fashion to the Blackberry, Ume, Shiso Shrub (page 191) and Ginger Strawberry Shrub (page 189). With respect to this particular pairing, I love how turmeric's floral, fruity, earthy, and peppery notes contrast with the pineapple's sweet, fragrant, and tropical flavor. If you are at a staid gathering, you can always liven things up by adding vodka, rum, tequila, or any other alcohol of choice.

Note: Fresh turmeric, a member of the ginger family native to India and Southeast Asia, can be found in specialty, gourmet, or Asian markets. I strongly recommend using the fresh variety over its dried cousin if possible, to capitalize on its much more robust flavor.

1 cup chopped fresh pineapple, plus more (optional) for garnish

3 tablespoons peeled, chopped fresh turmeric, or 1 tablespoon ground turmeric

¼ cup water

1 cup champagne vinegar

1 cup sugar

Ice cubes for serving

Sparkling water for serving

Place the pineapple, turmeric, and water in a blender and blend until smooth, about 1 minute. Set aside.

Combine the vinegar and sugar in a small saucepan and bring to a boil over high heat. Turn off the heat.

Pour the pineapple mixture into the vinegar and stir to combine, then push the mixture through a fine-mesh strainer over a measuring cup. Transfer to a clean bottle or jar and refrigerate until cold, 45 minutes to 1 hour.

To serve, pour a little of the shrub in a glass with ice and top with sparkling water.

Garnish with fresh pineapple, if desired. Store the shrub in the refrigerator for up to 1 month (top up and garnish just before serving).

SWEET LEMONGRASS-GINGER TEA

SERVES 4 TO 6 | ACTIVE TIME: 10 MINUTES

TOTAL TIME: 1 HOUR IF SERVING WARM OR 3 HOURS IF SERVING COLD

Rich in antioxidants, lemongrass brings us a bevy of health and detox benefits, from aiding digestion, boosting metabolism, and burning fat to bolstering the immune system. I've chosen it for this recipe for its fresh, citrusy, grassy snap, which nicely offsets the ginger's bite. This tea gets its sweetness from honey and can satisfy your urge for something sweet at the end of a meal in place of dessert.

Including a recipe for a hot tea in a cool-down cookbook is likely to cause a few double takes, I realize. But tea drinkers in Asia have long depended upon their hot, sweet sipping teas for thousands of years to help them cool down, and as recent studies have proven, there's a legitimate biological basis behind this practice. The tea's hot temperature—and in the case of this recipe, the spice from the ginger—induce sweat, and that's a good thing: our brains turn on the sweating mechanism to cool the body down. The only caveat is that the sweat must be able to evaporate—thus this approach will be more effective in hot and dry climates versus hot and humid ones (see page 60). However, if you make this tea and the weather turns humid, you need not panic, burst into tears, or blaspheme against your maker: just serve it over ice instead.

½ cup coarsely chopped fresh lemongrass

¾ cup coarsely chopped fresh ginger, skins and all

½ cup honey

8 cups water

¹⁄₁₆ ounce loose-leaf black tea (about 1 tablespoon or 2 tea bags—Lipton works great)

Combine the lemongrass, ginger, honey, and water in a medium saucepan. Bring to a boil over high heat. Turn off the heat, add the tea in an infuser or tea bags, cover, and let steep for 10 minutes. Remove just the infuser, cover again, and continue to steep the lemongrass and ginger mixture for about 35 more minutes.

Pour the brewed tea over a fine-mesh strainer into a pitcher or bowl. Serve hot or transfer to the refrigerator and serve cold. The tea can be stored in a pitcher in the refrigerator for up to 3 days. Reheat on the stovetop or in the microwave.

FRESH MINT, CRANBERRY, APPLE TEA REFRESHER

SERVES 4 TO 6 | ACTIVE TIME: 10 MINUTES | TOTAL TIME: 1 HOUR 20 MINUTES

This mashup of tea, juice, fruit, and fresh mint is a little sweet, a little tart, and lightly effervescent and offers a refreshing, cooling finish, thanks to the mint. Trust me when I say that a tall glassful hits the spot after a session of gardening, exercising, swimming at the beach, or any other warm weather activity. Alternatively, dispense with the exercise altogether and just drink it sitting in a lounge chair—you can't lose with this stuff, basically. I sometimes make a double batch, first because it's so easy to chug after spending time out in the blazing heat, and second because this concoction happens to make a splendid cocktail base. If you're in a festive mood, add a few ice cubes and a few ounces of vodka and stir. Just be mindful—it goes down easy.

Note: Fresh cranberries can be hard to find outside of autumn, but they're typically available in the freezer section year-round; the frozen variety will work perfectly well for this recipe.

4 cups water

1 cup packed mint sprigs, plus more for garnish

1 cup frozen and thawed or fresh cranberries, plus more for garnish

1/16 ounce loose-leaf black tea (about 1 tablespoon or 2 tea bags—Lipton works great)

3 cups cold sparkling apple cider

1 sweet apple, such as Gala or Pink Lady, cored and thinly sliced

In a medium saucepan, bring the water to a boil over high heat. Add the mint, cranberries, and tea in an infuser or tea bags. Stir, cover, and let steep for about 10 minutes.

Remove the infuser or tea bags and transfer the mixture to the refrigerator to cool completely, about 1 hour.

Push the tea mixture through a fine-mesh strainer into a large pitcher or bowl and gently stir in the sparkling apple cider. Serve in glasses garnished with cranberries, apple slices, and sprigs of mint. The tea mixture can be stored in a pitcher in the refrigerator for up to 2 days. Once the sparkling cider is added, garnish and serve immediately.

WATERMELON, COCONUT, ALOE VERA COOLER

SERVES 4 | ACTIVE TIME: 10 MINUTES | TOTAL TIME: 10 MINUTES

Designed to hydrate, this healthy-tasting and lightly sweet cooler is perfect for replenishing lost fluids after being out in the hot sun, hiking, working out, swimming, etc. Not to be confused with coconut milk, coconut water is a clear liquid that is tapped from the center of young green coconuts. It possesses natural electrolytes and potassium that are good for rehydration and help to prevent muscle spasms.

I suspect what you're really wondering about, though, is the aloe vera. Most people know aloe as a medicinal plant with a gooey extract that feels good on sunburns. Which it is. But many are surprised to learn that aloe gel is edible (and/or drinkable) if prepared properly. Aloe bears a mild taste and is something of a cure-all, bringing antioxidant, anti-carcinogenic, and blood sugar–lowering properties, to cite just a few of its numerous health benefits. As a bonus, if you make this recipe, you'll likely wind up with extra aloe vera: keep it in the fridge to use in other cooking applications and/or to rub on your skin for relief in case you find yourself itchy, burned, swollen, or need to remove the tattooed initials of an ex.

1 whole aloe vera leaf

4 cups chopped seedless watermelon, chilled

1 teaspoon fresh lemon zest

3 tablespoons fresh lemon juice

3 cups cold coconut water

Wash and dry the aloe vera leaf. Lay it flat and cut off the bumpy edges that form a seam. Next, cut the skin off the flat sides to expose the clear, solid gel-like flesh in the middle. Chop the clear gel into small cubes.

Transfer the cubes to a fine-mesh strainer and run under cold water to remove any debris and yellow liquid (known as the latex, this liquid is not edible). Transfer 2 tablespoons of gel to the blender and set the rest aside in an airtight container. Add the watermelon, lemon zest, lemon juice, and coconut water to the blender and blend until smooth.

Spoon 1 teaspoon of aloe vera cubes into each of 4 tall glasses and top with some of the cooler. Serve cold. The cooler can be stored in a pitcher in the refrigerator for up to 2 days. Stir a few times before serving.

MEXICAN COFFEE FRAPPÉ

SERVES 4 TO 6 | ACTIVE TIME: 10 MINUTES | TOTAL TIME: 10 MINUTES

A fine illustration of the "necessity is the mother of invention" principle, this recipe came about one day when certain unexpected pests—I mean guests—dropped by, and I needed to whip up something quickly, on the fly. I happened to have about a half-pitcher of cold-brew coffee sitting around (for lots more on cold brew, see page 30)—not enough to serve my visitors, but a start. I sized up my fridge and cupboard for ingredients that a) could extend the beverage's volume sufficiently and b) would combine to form a harmonious outcome. Happily, this was one of those times when all the planets aligned and inspiration struck. Thus was born the Mexican Coffee Frappé, which received raves from all involved, thanks to its triad of traditional Mexican flavors: cocoa, vanilla, and cinnamon. As a treat for hot days, it is simple to blend up, sweet, and super-frothy. Perhaps most important, the jolt of caffeine it delivers is potent enough to propel the average person through a blazing day without damage to their batteries, tires, or cooling systems. This recipe was originally developed to use up leftover (room temperature) coffee, but cold also works; if using freshly brewed hot coffee, let it cool first.

3 cups brewed coffee or cold brew, at room temperature or chilled

½ cup sweetened condensed milk

2 tablespoons instant espresso powder

1 tablespoon unsweetened cocoa powder

1 teaspoon pure vanilla extract

½ teaspoon ground cinnamon, plus more for serving

2 cups ice cubes

Whipped cream for serving

Combine the coffee, condensed milk, espresso powder, cocoa powder, vanilla, cinnamon, and ice in a blender. Blend on high speed until smooth and very frothy.

Divide among glasses. Spoon some of the froth over the top of each glass. Top with whipped cream and a sprinkling of cinnamon, if desired. Serve immediately.

WINES FOR HOT WEATHER

While by no means a sommelier, I do appreciate thoughtful wine-food pairings, and the right crisp glass on a hot day can refresh and cool the very soul, as well as elevate even the trickiest summer fare into a special meal. This list reflects my personal experience and tastes while leaving room for exploring your own preferences. Generally speaking, these wines tend toward high acid and lower alcohol, meaning they are not super-heavy and won't put you out of commission if you decide to indulge in a midday glass.

ROSÉS

Rosés of any type are easy on the eyes and give off fragrant notes of berries and melon (see Red Grapefruit–Rose Sorbet, page 165). Made from a wide variety of red grapes from all over the globe, rosés spend less time in contact with their skins, resulting in varying pink hues. As for taste, it's important to look at what grapes were used. The color will also give you clues—the brighter and pinker, the likelier it is to be a fruit-forward, medium-bodied wine; as it gets darker, you can look for more characteristics similar to light red wines. More orange or brick red colors can mean more earthy notes and spices. The lighter your rosé, the drier it will be, similar to a crisp white wine.

WHITE WINE

Pinot Grigio and Sauvignon Blanc are both highly versatile hot-weather options—either pairs well with anything you want to eat on a summer day. One has notes of citrus, pear, apple, and sometimes honey, whereas the latter tends to be crisper and drier, with grassy and herbal flavors.

People have strong opinions regarding Rieslings. Some find them too syrupy and sweet, even though there are dry varieties out there (look for *Trocken*, German for "dry," on the label). Chilled dry Riesling makes for excellent hot-weather drinking, in part because it cuts through any richness and complements many aromatic seasonings and spicy foods.

One sometimes forgets that champagne pairs beautifully with many foods, including raw or chilled, steamed seafood, crispy fried anything, and rich desserts. Its effervescent qualities add a refreshing zing and cut through fat and richness. If too steep for your budget, Spanish cava is both more affordable and closer in flavor to champagne than prosecco, which is usually sweeter.

RED WINE

Not *all* red wines will put you down for a nap on a sunny day. Grignolino is a zesty varietal grown in the Piedmont region of Italy (though if you were to assert that its color is really more deep pink than red, you might have a point). Medium-bodied and tannic with notes of berry fruit and a slightly spicy finish, it's a simple, easy-drinking wine that can be served chilled, and is meant to be drunk while still fresh and young.

Pinot Noir (*pinot nero* in Italy) is beloved for a reason. Light and subtle, these reds are nonetheless filled with depth and personality, boasting complex flavors that tend to emerge gradually. Easy to find, these too can be served lightly chilled if not too tannic.

DESSERT WINE

Brachetto (or Brachetto d'Acqui) is a frizzante (lightly sparkling), slightly sweet red charmer from Piedmont. Light-bodied and bearing notes of raspberry and cherry, Brachettos are usually served lightly chilled.

Moscato D'asti is a lightly fizzy Italian dessert wine made from the moscato *bianco* grape. For me, its effervescent qualities and honey-like flavor make this an outstanding pairing for many desserts, especially fruity ones.

Sauternes, a French dessert wine from Bordeaux, is made from Sauvignon Blanc, Muscadelle, and Sémillon grapes. Its distinctive flavor evokes notes of ripe, sweet stone fruit and honey, balanced by a beautiful acidity. Try some with simple frozen berries or grapes (see page 168) if you need an after-dinner second wind.

THE FUN STUFF

When serving a chilled wine, take it out of the refrigerator a few minutes prior to serving so it's not ice-cold in the glass. Drinking wine too cold risks losing some of its complexities and more subtle flavors. In general, sparkling wines and champagne should be served about 40°F, whereas chilled wines should be doled out around 45°F. Also don't be afraid to chill your red wine, especially in the heat! Red wines with low tannins chill very nicely without losing complexity or flavor.

Rules aside, no one actually works for the wine police. I prefer my wine au naturel, but needs must when the devil drives, and wine should be enjoyed regardless of the humidity. Trendy day-drinking phenom frosé is essentially a granita made from rosé, sugar, lemon juice, and pureed frozen fruit, including peaches, raspberries, or strawberries. Choose a dark pink rosé, as any wine will lose a bit of potency in freezing. The spritzer, while definitely a throwback, is a nice option if your white wine is on the heavy side for sipping by the pool or, horror, at room temperature. Combine equal parts white wine and extra-cold club soda over ice, with a twist of lemon or lime. When entertaining, add refreshing touches to simple drinks with aromatic herbal garnishes, fruit juice, or infused ice cubes (see page 208).

GRAPEFRUIT AND ROSEMARY SPRITZ

SERVES 4 | ACTIVE TIME: 15 MINUTES | TOTAL TIME: 15 MINUTES

This cold, fizzy, pertly refreshing cocktail spritz might as well have come out of *Mad Men* or *Breakfast at Tiffany's*. It checks all of the sensory boxes, offering a heady mix of the visual (lovely soft pink hue), the olfactory (aromatic peels of grapefruit muddled with woodsy rosemary, plus citrusy lime juice), the tactile and auditory (fizzy seltzer and frosty, tinkly ice cubes), and, of course, the gustatory (sweet-sour-bitter and oh-so-fresh-citrus). For alcohol I've opted for a combination of gin and Lillet, an aperitif made from a blend of Bordeaux wines and citrus liqueur that pairs perfectly with the fresh citrus juices and piney-flavored gin.

A brief word here on the health benefits of rosemary, which turns out to be a panacea for practically anything that ails you, if the nutritionists are to be believed. It reduces inflammation, protects the immune system, helps stimulate circulation, detoxifies the body, protects against bacterial infections, delays aging, heals many skin conditions, and relieves pain. Admittedly, if you drink enough of these spritzes, you won't be feeling that much pain to begin with.

6 fresh rosemary sprigs, plus more for garnish

4 long strips grapefruit peel from 1 grapefruit (made using a vegetable peeler), plus more for garnish

2 tablespoons sugar

1 cup fresh ruby red grapefruit juice

2 tablespoons fresh lime juice

6 ounces white Lillet

2 ounces gin

Ice cubes for serving

Seltzer water for serving

Using a mortar and pestle, grind the rosemary, grapefruit peel, and sugar together until the rosemary is pulverized and the oils from the grapefruit and rosemary are released. The mixture should smell very fragrant.

Place ½ cup ice in a cocktail shaker. Spoon the sugar mixture over the ice cubes. Top with the grapefruit juice, lime juice, Lillet, and gin. Shake until cold, then strain into 4 lowball glasses filled with ice. Slide a strip of zest down into each glass so that it wraps around the ice and makes a diagonal shape, then top each with seltzer and garnish with rosemary sprigs. Serve immediately.

WHITE GRAPE AND ELDERFLOWER BOOZY SLUSHIE

SERVES 2 | ACTIVE TIME: 5 MINUTES | TOTAL TIME: 5 MINUTES

When I was little, one of my favorite summer snacks was miniature, sweet, self-contained, no-stick ice pops—sometimes also referred to as "frozen grapes." Remembering how I loved to pop these in my mouth on hot days, I froze a bunch of white grapes last summer for our daughter to snack on. She quickly and unceremoniously rejected them, disabusing me of any sentimental notions of a new family tradition passing down through the generations. So I decided to update the old "when life hands you lemons, make lemonade" cliché (and soothe my bruised feelings while I was at it), by updating it with the following piece of modern wisdom, which I continue to stand by: *When life hands you rejected frozen grapes, make an adult beverage.*

As it turned out, I loved the adult beverage in question so much that I've included it in this book. Essentially it is a light green, smooth and refreshing, fragrant and frosty, alcoholic slushie that features both vodka and elderflower liqueur. The vodka provides the kick, and the elderflower liquor complements the flavor of the grapes with notes of fresh flowers, honey, grape, lychee, and quince. Because the frozen grapes serve as ice cubes, no dilution occurs, helping to take the edge off in the heat.

3 cups frozen white grapes

4 ounces elderflower liqueur, such as St-Germain

2 ounces vodka

2 tablespoons fresh lemon juice

Place the grapes, elderflower liqueur, vodka, and lemon juice in a high-powered blender and blend on high speed until smooth. Pour into glasses and serve immediately.

PEACH PLUM PEAR SANGRIA

SERVES 6 TO 8 | ACTIVE TIME: 12 MINUTES | TOTAL TIME: 2 HOURS

Isn't it about time that sangria—traditionally a dark red beverage made with red wine, brandy, and perhaps citrus fruit—is allowed a glimpse of the lighter side of life? This recipe provides just such an opportunity, with its foundation of rosé and summer fruits topped with fruity liqueurs and white grape juice. The result is a light pink sangria busting out all over with floral, fruity, and fragrant flavors. With respect to the fruit, I've used peach, plum, and pear here, but I grant you full license to play around based on your personal preference and whatever's in season. As with all sangrias, the longer the fruit sits, the more the flavor develops, so consider making this one at least a few hours before serving—better yet, a day.

Note: When cutting any soft, ripe fruit, using a serrated knife will save you a world of heartache.

2 tablespoons sugar

2 ounces Japanese plum wine

2 ounces pear vodka

2 ounces peach liqueur

1 cup white grape juice

1 peach (white or yellow), pitted and thinly sliced, plus more for garnish

1 plum, pitted and thinly sliced, plus more for garnish

1 Anjou pear, pitted and thinly sliced, plus more for garnish

2 sprigs fresh thyme, plus more for garnish

1 (750-ml) bottle rosé

Ice cubes for serving

In a small measuring cup, stir together the sugar, plum wine, pear vodka, peach liqueur, and white grape juice until the sugar dissolves.

Add the fruit and thyme to a large pitcher or bowl. Add the liqueur mixture and rosé and stir to combine. Refrigerate for at least 2 hours, overnight, or even up to 2 days. The longer the sangria sits, the more flavorful it becomes.

Serve the sangria over ice garnished with sliced peaches, plums, pears, and sprigs of thyme.

MIXED CITRUS PALOMA

SERVES 2 | ACTIVE TIME: 10 MINUTES | TOTAL TIME: 1 HOUR 15 MINUTES

Although *paloma* means "dove" in Spanish, this cocktail's name more likely derives from its color; per *Merriam-Webster*, paloma is a brownish orange to light brown hue, redder and lighter than sorrel, just the sort of hue that might emerge, if one were, say, to mix tequila gold with grapefruit pink. Indeed, the classic paloma is a fizzy Mexican cocktail that combines fresh grapefruit with lime, tequila, and soda. It's often served on the rocks, with a margarita-like salt rim on the glass, although a popular no-frills "workingman's" variation also exists, which apparently consists solely of tequila and grapefruit soda and is enjoyed straight from the can. No judgment—I'd gladly try either version on a hot day. However, my own twist (no pun intended) on the paloma includes fresh clementine (or tangerine) and lemon juices along with grapefruit. The upshot is a sweet, tart, tangy, bubbly, bright, and fresh cocktail that will help you remain *tranquilo* in adverse conditions—hot or otherwise.

Note: Prior to juicing your citrus, you will be using a vegetable peeler to remove the outer rind. Don't toss that peel! It will be used both to flavor the syrup and to garnish the cocktail.

Peels from the following (removed with a vegetable peeler): 1 clementine or tangerine, 1 ruby red grapefruit, and 1 lemon

½ cup sugar

½ cup water

½ cup fresh clementine or tangerine juice (from 8 clementines or 6 tangerines)

½ cup fresh ruby red grapefruit juice (from 1 to 2 grapefruits)

¼ cup fresh lemon juice (from 2 lemons)

4 ounces good-quality tequila (½ cup)

Ice cubes for serving

Seltzer water or Orangina for serving

Place the combined peel in a small saucepan along with the sugar and water. Bring to a simmer over medium heat, about 6 minutes. Continue to simmer until the sugar dissolves and the citrus peels take on a slight transparency, about 8 more minutes. Transfer the mixture with the peels in it to a large bowl or measuring cup and refrigerate until cold, about 1 hour.

Stir the clementine, grapefruit, and lemon juices and tequila into the sugar-and-peel mixture.

Divide the mixture evenly, including the peels, among tall glasses filled with ice. Top each with some seltzer water or Orangina. Serve immediately.

INFUSED ICE CUBES

I love infused ice cubes for the multitude of purposes they serve: they add interesting flavors, they increase visual interest, and, most important, they make our beverages ice-cold without dilution. The suggestions below should start you on the path to infused ice nirvana—and hopefully they'll inspire you to try your own variations. If you want to get more creative still, consider customizing your cube shapes and sizes. There's a dizzying variety of ice cube trays out there these days, with uses ranging from silly (e.g., skull-shaped cubes for Halloween parties) to serious (e.g., large single cubes for single malt scotch on the rocks).

JOLT CUBES

Combine 1 cup freshly brewed coffee with 2 tablespoons instant espresso powder and whisk to combine. Fill an ice cube tray and freeze until solid, about 4 hours or overnight. Use in place of regular ice cubes to ensure that your iced coffee, Overnight Cold Brew (page 30), or iced espresso drink retains its caffeinated kick, or replace the ice in the Mock Vanilla Milkshake (page 12) with some jolt cubes for an adult version of the drink.

CREAMY DREAMY CUBES

Add 2 tablespoons sweetened condensed milk to every 1 cup whole milk and whisk until smooth. Pour into an ice cube tray and freeze until solid, about 4 hours or overnight. Use these in place of milk in any coffee drink, strong black iced tea, or Thai iced tea.

SPA CUBES

Thinly slice and chop lemon and cucumber and place in the cups of an ice cube tray. Fill with water and freeze until solid, about 4 hours or overnight. Place the ice cubes in glasses of filtered water for that fancy spa effect. Try adding some spa cubes to the Watermelon, Coconut, Aloe Vera Cooler (page 197).

FLOWER POWER CUBES

Place edible flower petals and berries in an ice cube tray. Fill with water and freeze until solid, about 4 hours or overnight. Place in glasses, top with filtered water, fruity or herbal iced tea, fruit juice, or seltzer water, and let the oohs and aahs commence. Try adding these to the Hibiscus, Rosehip, and Berry Agua Fresca (page 186) or the Fresh Mint, Cranberry, Apple Tea Refresher (page 194).

"MARY POP-INS" CUBES

Spoon ¼ teaspoon prepared horseradish into each cup of an ice cube tray. Cover with tomato juice, stir with a small spoon, and freeze until solid, about 4 hours or overnight. Fill tall glasses with the "Mary Pop-ins" and top with a Bloody Mary mix, vodka, and lemon.

PINEAPPLE, THYME, AND COCONUT WATER WHIP

SERVES 4 | ACTIVE TIME: 5 MINUTES | TOTAL TIME: 5 MINUTES

If you like piña coladas and getting caught in the rain (as the song goes), this recipe may not be for you. True, it may be reminiscent of the piña colada in some ways, but its primary emphasis is on pineapple and fresh thyme, the latter of which gives the drink an unexpected herbal twist. Additionally, unlike the super-rich coconut crème (or crema de coco) typically used in the piña colada, my drink uses mildly sweet coconut water, which is far less fatty—a distinct plus during a heat wave (and a good source of natural electrolytes, to boot).

Overall, this recipe boasts many of the colada assets (frothiness, smooth and creamy texture, tropical feel) while avoiding some of its liabilities (calorific heaviness, nap-inducing quality). True, you may not wind up making love at midnight, in the dunes of the cape, but is that really desirable when the tick population is exploding and the thermometer is pushing 100? Call me unromantic, but personally, the escape I'm looking for under such conditions is from the heat itself.

Note: You can buy frozen pineapple in the freezer section of your local supermarket. Better still, if you have the time and the fruit, freeze your own (see page 168) in advance—just remember it takes the freezer a few hours to do its thing.

2 cups chopped frozen pineapple (see headnote)

1 cup coconut water

3 ounces white rum

5 tablespoons fresh lime juice

2 tablespoons sugar

½ teaspoons fresh thyme leaves, plus sprigs for garnish

Pineapple wedges for garnish

Combine the frozen pineapple, coconut water, rum, lime juice, sugar, and thyme leaves in a blender and blend on high speed until very frothy.

Divide the whip among 4 glasses. Garnish with a fresh thyme sprig and a wedge of pineapple. Serve immediately.

WATERMELON, JALAPEÑO, AND SALT CAIPIRINHAS

SERVES 4 | ACTIVE TIME: 8 MINUTES | TOTAL TIME: 8 MINUTES

When the weather is hot in Brazil—and depending on what Brazilian region, that may mean the majority of the year—it's caipirinha time. Caipirinhas are traditionally made with just three simple ingredients: lime, sugar, and cachaça. Available at most liquor stores, cachaça is somewhat reminiscent of rum, but brings its own unique flavor (rum being made from molasses and cachaça from sugar cane). Here I've thrown in a few wild cards to up the hot-weather-relief ante—namely watermelon, spicy jalapeño, and a bit of salt as a flavor enhancer. Just be careful—caipirinhas go down easy, and cachaça packs a punch (i.e., it may be best to wait until after your capoeira lesson).

4 cups chopped seedless watermelon
(from 1 small seedless watermelon)

3 tablespoons thinly sliced jalapeño chile, divided

½ cup fresh lime juice

3 tablespoons sugar

4 ounces (½ cup) cachaça

¾ teaspoon sea salt

Ice cubes for serving

Place the watermelon, 1 tablespoon of the jalapeño, the lime juice, and sugar in a blender and blend on high speed until smooth.

Push the watermelon juice mixture with a silicone spatula through a fine-mesh strainer over a large measuring cup or pitcher. Stir in the cachaça and salt.

Fill 4 medium cocktail glasses with ice and divide the remaining 2 tablespoons jalapeño slices among them. Strain the caipirinhas into the 4 glasses. Serve immediately.

PANTRY

QUICK AND SPICY MEDITERRANEAN LEMON PICKLES

MAKES 3 CUPS PICKLES, PLUS BRINE | ACTIVE TIME: 5 MINUTES | TOTAL TIME: 25 MINUTES

Traditional lemon pickles, which originated in India and North Africa, can take months to make. That's because pickled lemons typically are not cooked, but rather sliced, salted, jarred, and left to ferment. The result is worth it, though: a tangy, spicy, and salty condiment with a briny and bright flavor that makes them a splendid, exotic substitute for—or companion to—olives. (Speaking of which, next time you're in the mood for a martini, try adding a slice of lemon pickle rind and some lemon pickle juice to the mix. If you don't like it, I'll drink it.)

For those without months to spare, this recipe will allow you to make a quite tasty version in just a fraction of the time, thanks to some brief boiling. That said, they last for two to three months in your fridge, and only get better as the weeks pass. And yes, you can and should eat the peel. Several recipes in this book make use of these pickles, such as the Grilled Marinated Skirt Steak and Barley Salad with Dried Cherries, Fresh Herbs, and Lemon Pickle (page 149) and the Spicy Chickpea and Herb Salad over Olive Oil Labneh (page 69). Finally, they appear in the Salted Lemon Semifreddo (page 177)—but definitely omit the chile and oregano when pickling lemons for this recipe (or another sweet application)!

4 whole lemons, washed well and dried

3 tablespoons sugar

3 tablespoons sea salt

1 cup water

1 serrano, Fresno, or jalapeño chile, stem removed and sliced

2 sprigs fresh oregano

Halve each lemon crosswise, then cut each half into 8 (1-inch) pieces and place in a medium saucepan.

Add the sugar, salt, and water. Stir to combine and bring to a boil over medium heat. When a rolling boil is reached (after about 7 minutes), reduce the heat to a simmer. Cook until the lemon skin is tender, 12 to 14 minutes.

Transfer to a bowl to cool slightly, then stir in the chile and oregano (omit this step if using the lemons in a sweet application; see headnote). Store in an airtight container in the refrigerator for up to 3 months.

MIDDLE EASTERN TURNIP AND BEET PICKLES

MAKES 3 CUPS PICKLES, PLUS BRINE | ACTIVE TIME: 15 MINUTES | TOTAL TIME: 1 HOUR

One of my favorite elements of the sizzling Middle Eastern gyro or falafel platter is the small mound of cold, bright-colored magenta beet and turnip pickles you often get as an accompaniment. Sometimes you don't, though, which I always find decidedly disappointing. As a precautionary measure against such a catastrophe, I've started making my own version to have at the ready. Their briny, sweet, salty, and tart flavor is perfect for cutting through any hot and rich food; try serving some alongside the Grilled Marinated Skirt Steak and Barley Salad with Dried Cherries, Fresh Herbs, and Lemon Pickle (page 149), for example, or the Middle Eastern Crunch Salad (page 66).

1 large turnip (about 12 ounces), peeled and cut into 1½-inch pieces

1 medium beet (about 4 ounces), peeled and cut into 1-inch cubes

1¼ cups unseasoned rice vinegar

½ cup water

2 teaspoons sea salt

1 tablespoon sugar

3 juniper berries

Place the turnip, beet, vinegar, water, salt, sugar, and juniper berries in a medium saucepan over medium heat.

Bring just to a boil, about 7 minutes, then turn off the heat. Transfer to a medium bowl to cool slightly, then refrigerate in an airtight container until cold. Use right away or keep refrigerated in an airtight container for up to 4 weeks.

GARLICKY PICKLED RED CABBAGE

MAKES 2½ CUPS PICKLES, PLUS BRINE | ACTIVE TIME: 10 MINUTES | TOTAL TIME: 1 HOUR

Brightly flavored, briny, and garlicky, these magenta-colored pickled cabbage strands make a perfect addition to anything crying out for an extra bit of flavor, acid, and/or crunch. They're great on top of salads, for example—and will add pizzazz to grain bowls, sandwiches, and tacos of any stripe. The observant may notice that this item is featured in two other recipes in this book, the better to take advantage of its vinegary, bright notes and—full disclosure—its photogenic color. They also make a delicious snack on their own, eaten with a fork straight out of the jar, not that you'd find me indulging in such barbaric behavior, at least not in front of company.

2 cups shredded red cabbage
(about ½ medium head of cabbage)

2½ teaspoons sea salt

¾ cup unseasoned rice vinegar

2 teaspoons coriander seeds

3 cloves garlic, peeled and thinly sliced

1 tablespoon sugar

Place the cabbage in a large nonreactive bowl. Sprinkle with the salt and massage the salt into the cabbage. Set aside.

In a small saucepan, stir together the vinegar, coriander seeds, garlic, and sugar. Bring to a boil over high heat, about 3 minutes.

Pour the vinegar mixture over the cabbage and stir to combine. Let sit, stirring occasionally, until the pickles are room temperature, then store in an airtight container in the refrigerator for up to 1 month, until ready to use.

BROCCOLI AND CARROT GINGER PICKLES

MAKES 3½ CUPS PICKLES, PLUS BRINE | ACTIVE TIME: 15 MINUTES | TOTAL TIME: 1 HOUR

I realize I'm in the minority here, but I've always preferred crunchy broccoli stems over the tender florets. That's why I can be spotted on occasion combing through mounds of broccoli in the produce section—I'm searching for the heads with extra-long stems. If this causes amusement among my fellow shoppers, I'm consoled by knowing that I will have the last laugh, for these stems will soon be sliced thin and tossed into stir-fries, frittatas, or pasta sauces. Or else—perhaps you can guess where I'm going with this one—pickled. In this combo, I love how the fragrant tones and a bit of heat from the ginger complement the sweetness of the carrots and slightly bitter, robust, earthy broccoli. Besides being natural on sandwiches (see page 104), savvy eaters use these pickles to top salads or to accompany—and cut though—fried seafood, ribs, burgers, or other rich and fatty fare. Try them as a tangy, crunchy addition to an easy seafood spread (see page 120).

An earlier incarnation of this recipe called for the veggies to be sliced thinly by hand, but I found that it took ages, and the pickles were still too thick for my liking. So—in a moment of inspiration—I took out my serrated vegetable peeler and went at it. I loved the result—pickled zoodles, if you will. A veggie spiralizer makes an excellent alternative, too, by the way. If you are among the hordes of home chefs who have had a spiralizer sitting idly in your drawer for years, have a heart. Let it see the light of day and do what it was put on God's green earth to do.

10 ounces broccoli stems (about 5 stems from 1 large bunch)

8 ounces carrots (about 2 large carrots)

2 cups apple cider vinegar

½ cup water

¼ cup sugar

2 teaspoons sea salt

1 ounce fresh ginger, peeled and julienned (about ¼ cup)

Use a vegetable peeler or paring knife to remove the woody outer layer of the broccoli stems. Use a serrated vegetable peeler or vegetable spiralizer to slice the broccoli into long, thin strands until you have about 2 cups broccoli strands. Repeat the process with the carrots until you have about 2 cups carrots. Save any vegetable scraps for another use. Place the broccoli and carrots in a medium bowl and set aside.

In a small saucepan, stir together the vinegar, water, sugar, and salt. Bring the vinegar mixture to a simmer over high heat, about 3 minutes. Add the ginger and bring to a boil.

Turn off the heat and the pour the vinegar mixture over the broccoli and carrots. Use tongs to toss the mixture in the vinegar, then let cool to room temperature, about 45 minutes.

Transfer to an airtight container or jar and store in the refrigerator for up to 1 month.

PICKLED GINGER

MAKES 2 CUPS PICKLES, PLUS BRINE | ACTIVE TIME: 10 MINUTES | TOTAL TIME: 1 HOUR 20 MIINUTES

The first time I pickled my own ginger was for a poke party (see page 126). Long story short, guests were on the way, we were out of pickled ginger, and the supermarket was closed. We did have fresh ginger, though—so drawing on the same spirit the Pilgrims would have shown had they been out of ginger at a poke party—I decided to pickle my own, and to this day, I've continued to pickle ginger as per the recipe below. It's quite simple—the only tricky part is slicing the ginger extra thin. Once pickled, it can sit in your fridge for up to two months in an airtight container. Refreshingly cold, sweet, and slightly spicy, it cuts through any rich, fatty food and cools the taste buds. Try pickled ginger not just with poke, sushi, or *tamago* (see page 22), but also cooked salmon. You can even use the pickling liquid as you would a shrub—combined with a splash of seltzer water over ice or tipped into cocktails or mocktails.

8 ounces fresh ginger

1 cup sugar

1 cup rice wine vinegar

Cut any knobby ends off the ginger, then peel—reserve these materials for the Sweet Lemongrass-Ginger Tea (page 193).

Very thinly slice the ginger $\frac{1}{16}$ to $\frac{1}{8}$ inch thick with a sharp chef's knife or mandoline (this is something you'll get better at with practice, but the recipe works whether or not the ginger is sliced paper-thin). You should have about 1½ cups sliced ginger.

Place the sugar, vinegar, and ginger in a small saucepan and bring to a boil over high heat, about 3 minutes.

Reduce the heat to low, stir, and continue to cook until the ginger softens, about 10 more minutes. Transfer to a medium bowl to cool to room temperature, about 1 hour. Transfer the ginger and pickling juices to an airtight container and store refrigerated for up to 2 months.

SPICY DAIKON PICKLES

MAKES 3 CUPS PICKLES | ACTIVE TIME: 12 MINUTES | TOTAL TIME: 1 HOUR

These pickles first came to my attention as part of a banchan—petite dishes of condiments and salads that traditionally accompany Korean BBQ. Served cold, these crunchy daikon pickles are a great antidote to anything warm and remotely rich (like Korean BBQ), the secret being the vibrant, salty, pungent, gingery flavor, which asserts itself and acts as a foil to counterbalance fatty foods. Daikon, a member of the radish family, is large and white, mild, and remains crunchy even when pickled. Quick to make, they go well with just about any entree of Asian pedigree. Try them, for example, with the Cold Korean-Style Vegetable Noodles with Gochujang and Kimchi (page 131). Last, served alongside pretty much anything deep-fried, Asian or otherwise, these pickles will contribute positively to your meal.

1 pound daikon, peeled and cut into 1-inch cubes (about 3 cups)

1 tablespoon peeled and chopped fresh ginger

2 to 3 moderately hot to hot chiles (to taste), such as Fresno or Thai, stems removed and roughly chopped

3 cloves garlic, smashed with the side of a chef's knife and peeled

¾ cup rice vinegar

2 tablespoons sugar

½ cup Thai fish sauce

Place the daikon in a medium bowl.

Combine the ginger, chiles, and garlic in a food processor and process until very finely chopped, about 2 minutes.

In a small saucepan over high heat, bring the rice vinegar and sugar just to a boil, about 3 minutes. Stir in the ginger, chiles, garlic, and fish sauce.

Pour the mixture over the daikon. Stir to coat and bring to room temperature. Store refrigerated in an airtight container for up to 1 month.

HERBY PISTOU

MAKES 1 CUP | ACTIVE TIME: 10 MINUTES | TOTAL TIME: 10 MINUTES

You could be forgiven for assuming that *pistou*—this vibrant, fragrant, green, herby, Provençal sauce—is going to be a French variation on pesto, since it looks (and sounds) so similar. Also because it actually is a French variation on pesto. Loaded with fresh herbs, garlic, lemon, and olive oil, pistou's primary distinction from its Italian cousin is simply that it has no nuts and less cheese (sometimes no cheese at all if making a vegan version). Accordingly, it's a bit lighter and brighter than pesto, and thus makes for an excellent hot weather stand-in. I find that the addition of pistou is an easy way to make something mundane seem more upscale (and, more important, to make it taste better). Its uses are many: serve it as is, alongside a plate crudités for dipping, as an extra served next to the Spicy Grilled Eggplant Romesco Dip (page 36), or as part of an easy seafood spread (see page 120); stir a teaspoon or two into a bowl of soup, such as the Red Gazpacho (page 83) or Cauliflower, Pea, and Leek Soup Topped with Heirloom Tomatoes, Pea Tendrils, and Olive Oil (page 91); or spoon a dollop onto a grain bowl—try it with the Grilled Marinated Skirt Steak and Barley Salad with Dried Cherries, Fresh Herbs, and Lemon Pickle (page 149), for example. You can also mix a bit of mayo into pistou to quickly conjure up a creamy-herby spread for a sandwich, or add a dollop on top of the Grilled Shrimp with Herb Butter and Arugula on Ciabatta Toast (page 111).

2 cups packed fresh basil leaves

1 cup packed fresh flat-leaf parsley

⅓ cup packed fresh mint leaves

1 tablespoon fresh thyme leaves or lemon thyme, if available

1 tablespoon fresh oregano leaves

2 cloves garlic, smashed with the side of a chef's knife and peeled

1 tablespoon fresh lemon zest

2 tablespoons fresh lemon juice

2 tablespoons grated Parmigiano-Reggiano cheese

⅓ cup extra virgin olive oil

Sea salt

Freshly ground black pepper

In the bowl of a food processor, combine the basil, parsley, mint, thyme, oregano, garlic, lemon zest, lemon juice, and cheese and pulse until finely chopped, about 30 times.

With the motor running, slowly drizzle in the olive oil and process until the herbs are finely chopped (but not pureed). Season with salt and pepper. Store refrigerated in an airtight container with an additional thin layer of oil (for no air contact) for up to 3 days.

MANGO CARROT AMBA

MAKES 3 CUPS | ACTIVE TIME: 25 MINUTES | TOTAL TIME: 25 MINUTES

Traditional amba—a pureed mango condiment with a spicy, briny flavor—can sometimes be found in jarred versions at international markets, spice stores, and gourmet shops. However, while buying the jarred variety is a time saver, it just doesn't compare to the real, homemade stuff. My recipe supplements mango with carrot to mellow out the sauce's sharpness and add a bit of sweetness. Savory, sweet, tart, and spicy in equal measures, this sauce makes a great addition to a pita platter, meat sandwich, grilled fish, or any type of grain bowl and its beautiful, sunny hue livens up any plate. Pro tip: Add oil, vinegar, and a little water for a divine salad dressing.

¼ cup canola oil

2 teaspoons cumin seeds

1 teaspoon yellow mustard seeds

1 teaspoon coriander seeds

½ teaspoon fenugreek seeds

1 small shallot, peeled and chopped (about ¼ cup)

3 cloves garlic, peeled and finely chopped

2 tablespoons finely chopped peeled fresh turmeric or 1 tablespoon ground turmeric

1 Fresno chile, stem removed and thinly sliced

3 cups coarsely chopped ripe mango, from about 2 whole mangos (peeled and pitted)

1 cup shredded carrot (from 2 large carrots)

¼ cup apple cider vinegar

½ cup water

Sea salt

Freshly ground black pepper

In a medium saucepan, warm the canola oil over medium-low heat until shimmering, about 2 minutes. Add the cumin seeds, mustard seeds, and coriander seeds and cook, stirring occasionally, until fragrant and lightly toasted, about 2 minutes.

Add the fenugreek seeds, shallot, garlic, turmeric (if fresh), and chile. Cook, stirring occasionally, until the shallot begins to soften, about 2 minutes. If using dried turmeric, stir it in at this point.

Stir in the mango, carrot, vinegar, and water. Bring to a simmer and cook until the carrot has softened, about 7 minutes total.

Transfer the mixture to a food processor or high-powered blender and process until smooth, about 2 minutes. Season with salt and pepper. Let cool to room temperature, then transfer to an airtight container and refrigerate until ready to use. The amba will last about 1 month in the refrigerator.

TOASTED GARLIC, GINGER, AND CHILE OIL

MAKES ⅔ CUP | ACTIVE TIME: 25 MINUTES | TOTAL TIME: 45 MINUTES

This crunchy, toasty, highly flavorful oil is full of delicious crispy bits and great on just about anything. I first came across a similar condiment years ago at a dim sum restaurant in lower Manhattan. It added great flavor and a bit of heat to any dumpling it touched. Thinly sliced garlic, ginger, and chiles get bathed and toasted in oil and then finely chopped in a food processor. Sugar, vinegar, and salt are added to liven things up even more. I love this oil and the irresistible crispy bits on any Asian-inspired rice or noodle dish, but it also works wonders stirred into a bowl of soup, drizzled on a salad, or spooned over a bowl of rice or grains. The uses are endless!

½ cup peeled and thinly sliced cloves garlic (about 8 cloves total)

¼ cup thinly sliced stemmed Fresno chiles (from 2 chiles)

1 tablespoon thinly sliced peeled fresh ginger (from about a 1-inch knob)

½ cup canola oil or any other neutral-flavored oil

1 teaspoon sugar

½ teaspoon sea salt

1 teaspoon unseasoned rice vinegar

Off the heat, stir together the garlic, chiles, ginger, and canola oil in a small saucepan.

Transfer to the stovetop and cook over medium heat, stirring occasionally, until the garlic is golden brown, 9 to 15 minutes (go carefully so as not to burn the garlic, but it does take a little time to get properly golden and crispy).

Immediately transfer the mixture, including the oil, to the bowl of a food processor. Let stand to cool slightly, about 20 minutes, then add the sugar, salt, and vinegar and pulse about 15 times, until coarsely chopped. Store in an airtight container in the refrigerator for up to 1 month.

SPICY PEPPER JELLY

MAKES 1 CUP | ACTIVE TIME: 15 MINUTES | TOTAL TIME: 1 HOUR

Pepper jelly is an old-school preserve that imparts a spicy and sweet kick to whatever it touches. Typically it's made with sugar, pectin, vinegar, and some form of hot or semi-hot peppers. I've always been a fan, and whenever I see a jar I'm tempted to buy it, but I try to remind myself that it's simple to make and the minimal effort involved pays handsomely in terms of the flavor and freshness upgrade that homemade delivers. If you want proof, try the pepper jelly recipe below. Regarding usage, most often you see it paired with meats—especially as a sandwich condiment— or served on crackers with cream cheese as an appetizer. However, its versatility is such that it's well worth keeping around in your pantry: I also recommend slathering this jelly on buttered toast, stirring a little into a salad dressing, or even adding some to an otherwise plain grilled cheese sandwich. I have included it as part of the Pan-Seared Pork Sandwich with Spicy Papaya Slaw and Spicy Pepper Jelly on Sourdough (page 115).

1 red bell pepper, stem removed, seeded, and coarsely chopped (about 1¼ cups)

1 to 2 Fresno chiles (depending on heat desired), stems removed and chopped

1 cup sugar

4 teaspoons powdered pectin

2 tablespoons apple cider vinegar

Place the bell pepper, chiles, and sugar in the bowl of a food processor and process until very smooth, about 1 minute.

Transfer the mixture to a medium saucepan. Stir in the pectin and bring to a boil over medium-high heat, about 4 minutes.

Continue to boil, stirring a few times, until thickened slightly, 4 to 6 minutes. Take off the heat and stir in the vinegar. Transfer to a medium bowl and let cool to room temperature, then transfer to the refrigerator to cool completely. The jelly will last in an airtight container in the refrigerator for up to 1 month.

RAITA

MAKES ABOUT 2 CUPS | ACTIVE TIME: 15 MINUTES | TOTAL TIME: 25 MINUTES

If you eat lots of spicy food, especially chiles, you probably know one of the worst things to turn to for relief is cold water. Water only spreads around the capsaicin—the waxy compound that gives peppers heat, which tends to coat the tongue—thus increasing the radius of the nuclear meltdown in your mouth. By delicious contrast, fat, oil, and dairy will dissolve capsaicin, which is why yogurt-based raita is commonly served alongside fiery vindaloos and spicy curries. My recipe incorporates cucumber, herbs, and toasted spices for depth of flavor and contrasting textures. Fresh curry leaves are becoming easier to find in well-appointed markets like Whole Foods, but you can also try a local Indian or South Asian grocer or look online.

1 seedless cucumber (about 12 ounces)

½ teaspoon sea salt, plus more to taste

1 cup whole milk plain yogurt

2 tablespoons extra virgin olive oil

¼ cup coarsely chopped fresh curry leaves

¼ teaspoon yellow mustard seeds

¼ teaspoon cumin seeds

¼ cup chopped fresh cilantro

2 tablespoons chopped fresh mint

Use a vegetable peeler to peel the cucumber. Then use a box grater to grate the entire cucumber. Place the grated cucumber in a fine-mesh strainer over a medium bowl. Stir ½ teaspoon salt into the cucumber and let drain and soften, about 10 minutes.

Use clean hands to squeeze any additional liquid from the cucumber. Discard the liquid, then transfer the cucumber to a medium bowl. Stir in the yogurt and set aside.

Heat the olive oil in a small skillet over medium-high heat until very hot and shimmering, about 3 minutes. Stir in the curry leaves, mustard seeds, and cumin seeds. Keep stirring until the mixture is lightly toasted and fragrant, with the seeds beginning to pop and the leaves becoming crispy, about 2 minutes. Take off the heat and immediately stir the mixture into the bowl with the yogurt. Add the cilantro and mint and stir to combine. Season with more salt, if desired. The raita can be stored in an airtight container in the refrigerator for up to 4 days.

CURED EGG YOLKS

MAKES 6 | ACTIVE TIME: 10 MINUTES | TOTAL TIME: ABOUT 1 WEEK

I became acquainted with cured egg yolks a few years ago when I noticed them on a restaurant menu; soon I started seeing them everywhere. The idea of them may sound strange at first. Cured egg yolks are bright yellow and possess a dense, gelatinous consistency that allows them to be grated over dishes as a sort of seasoning. They are somewhat akin to grated Parmigiano-Reggiano, in the sense that they add saltiness and a rich umami quality to whatever they touch, such as Chilled Borscht with Pumpernickel Croutons, Microgreens, Cream Cheese Foam, and Grated Cured Egg Yolk (page 94). They're also tremendous grated over toast with butter. Note: I find that a rasp-style grater helps better disperse the yolks over whatever I'm adding them to. Although the curing process is slow—it takes a little over a week—the work involved is minimal and no oven is required, always a plus in the hot weather. Cured eggs will last about one month in an airtight container in the refrigerator.

2 cups fine sea salt

¾ cup sugar

6 egg yolks

Mix the salt and sugar in a medium bowl. Pour half of the salt mixture into a wide, flat 8 by 12-inch baking dish.

Use a spoon to make 6 shallow indentations in the mixture.

Crack the eggs and separate the egg yolks from the egg whites. Place each yolk in one of the indentations. Save the egg whites for another use, or freeze in an airtight container until ready to use.

Gently spoon the remaining salt mixture over the yolks, covering them completely. Cover and refrigerate until the yolks feel solid, 5 days to 1 week.

Remove the yolks from the refrigerator and gently brush off some of the extra salt mixture, then discard the remaining salt mixture. Wrap each yolk loosely in cheesecloth and place on a cooling rack in a dry environment for 2 days. If your atmosphere is humid, place the egg yolks in an unheated oven for 2 days. Once firm and dried out, they are ready to use. Store in the cheesecloth in an airtight container in the refrigerator for up to 1 month.

Unwrap the yolks and use a fine grater to grate the cured egg yolk as desired over salads, soups, toast with butter, pasta, etc.

(Page references in *italics* refer to illustrations.)

ACKNOWLEDGMENTS

To say that creating a cookbook is not a one-person show is to make a huge understatement. Without the love, help, kindness, ideas and feedback, and dedicated technical contributions from my friends, family, and colleagues this book simply would not have been possible. My heartfelt thanks go out to the following:

My immediate family—husband, Jon, daughter, Katia, and cat, Birdie—for your love, support, ideas, and patience throughout this process and to Jon's second set of eyes, sense of humor, and incredible editing skills.

Rizzoli, for giving me the fantastic opportunity to pursue this idea, and especially to Jono Jarrett, my editor, for your ideas, positive energy, advice, brilliant prop suggestions and loaners, and for tweaking and shaping the book into what it has become.
Leda Scheintaub, who did great work copyediting.

My Relish&Co. team members and friends:
Stacey Cramp, for your keen eye and beautiful photography, lighting, and prop selections.
Jennifer S. Muller, for your art direction during our photoshoots and brilliant book design.

The recipe testers—Gillian Cridler, Hyeri Yoon, Fiona Brooks, and Rochelle Spiegel—
for your time, effort, taste buds, and honest opinions.

Our various family clans for your love, encouragement, and support—
Seder, Gustafson, Cotter, Pittel, and Gresham.

East Fork Pottery for their beautiful pottery loans.

Linda and John (and Waffles!) of Wary Meyers for your friendship, for the use of your home and pool at our photoshoot, and for your positive energies and kind spirits.

The Stonewall Kitchen Cooking School for guest chef and book signing opportunities and overall support.

The Portland Maine Farmers' Market farmers and vendors for helping grow and provide the beautiful produce used in developing the recipes and styling in this book.

My homes away from home: Portland Maine Whole Foods Market, Rosemont Markets, Hannaford Supermarkets, Sun Oriental, and H Mart for helping me fill this book with beautiful seasonal produce and exotic/international ingredients.

Both Bow Street Beverage and Browne Trading Company for helping me learn more about hot weather wines. Skordo and Gryffon Ridge Spice Merchants for your beautiful, high-quality selections of spices.

The Institute of Culinary Education for providing a strong cooking foundation—
I can't believe it's been sixteen years!

Vitamix for my incredible high-powered blender and Cuisinart for my tried and true workhorse of a food processor—both were indispensable when developing recipes for this book.

Kathleen and Will Pratt at Tandem Coffee Roasters for sharing the ultimate cold brew recipe!